HV
6250.4 Singh, Priyam, 1933–
W65
S54   Victims or criminals?
1996

DATE DUE

HV
6250.4 Singh, Priyam, 1933–
W65
S54   Victims or criminals?
1996

DATE	ISSUED TO
DEC 1 8 1999	

AUDREY COHEN COLLEGE LIBRARY
75 Varick St. 12th Floor
New York, NY 10013

VICTIMS OR CRIMINALS?

Women laborers, menials and outcasts have lived in hovels half-naked and half-hungry and have provided *hidden services* to support their families, the wealthy, the powerful, many nations and civilizations for centuries. They have been victims of worse forms of domestic violence, societal abuse and injustice. To them, and to all women victims of violence and injustice, this work is dedicated.

HV
6250.4
W65
S54
1996

VICTIMS OR CRIMINALS?

A Study of Women in
Colonial North-Western Provinces and
Oudh, India, 1870–1910

Priyam Singh

THE CASLON COMPANY

AUDREY COHEN COLLEGE LIBRARY
75 Varick St. 12th Floor
New York, NY 10013

First published in 1996 in the United States of America by
THE CASLON COMPANY
Middletown, New Jersey

© 1996 by Priyam Singh

Library of Congress Cataloging-in-Publication Data

Singh, Priyam, 1933–
  Victims or criminals? : a study of women in colonial North-Western Provinces and Oudh, India, 1870–1910 / Priyam Singh.
    p.   cm.
  Includes bibliographical references and index.
  ISBN 0-391-03971-7
  1. Women—India—United Provinces of Agra and Oudh—Crimes against. 2. Female offenders—India—United Provinces of Agra and Oudh. 3. Women—India—Untied Provinces of Agra and Oudh—Social conditions. 4. India—History—British occupation, 1765–1947.
I. Title.
HV6250.4.W65S54   1996
364.954'2—dc20   96-3782
                                                           CIP

All rights reserved. No part of this publication may be
reproduced or transmitted, in any form or by any means,
without written permission from the publisher.

Printed in the United States of America

CONTENTS

List of Tables vii

Acknowledgments ix

Preface xi

Introduction 1

1 Economic Deprivation and Women's Criminality 15

2 Patriarchy, Colonial Rulers, and Women Criminals 47

3 The Colonial State: Modernization or Demoralization of Women? 81

4 Colonial Justice, the Penal System, and Women Criminals 95

5 Conclusions 117

Appendices 127

   A: Cases of Reported Rapes and Low Percentage of Convictions 127

   B: Figures Showing the Religion and Age of Female Convicts 128

References 129

Index 141

LIST OF TABLES

1	Female Prisoners in Jails between 1876 and 1909	16
2	Female Population and Influx of Female Prisoners in Jails between 1876 and 1911	17
3	General Increase in the Crime Rate between 1876 and 1886	21
4	Population Growth of Allahabad, Jaunpur, Cawnpore, Fatehpur, Banda, and Hamirpur Districts between 1865 and 1881	24
5	Grain Thefts in Oudh, 1869–1875	25
6	Quinquennial Variations in Wage Rates for Cawnpore, Fyzabad, and Meerut	25
7	Variations in Quinquennial Average Cost of Common Food Grains, 1861–1898	27
8	Registered Population for 1872, 1881, 1891, 1901, 1911, and 1921	29
9	Number of Female Jail Population, Number Transported to Penal Colonies, and Number Executed between 1875 and 1912	49
10	Reported Attempted Suicide between 1871 and 1875	54
11	Hindu and Muslim Widows, Aged 9–14, 1882	62
12	Occupation of Female Convicts in Jails and Rate of Widowed Convicts	69

ACKNOWLEDGMENTS

I wish to acknowledge all those who have been instrumental in the completion of this study. Special thanks and recognition are due to Dr. Peter Gran for his invaluable guidance, advice, comments, and theoretical assistance. I received valuable guidance, suggestions, encouragement, and support from Dr. Thomas Patterson right through the period of my study. Dr. David Ludden provided constructive suggestions in locating references. His comments and criticism of my work from the beginning to the completion of this study was invaluable. I am grateful to them both. Thanks are also due to Dr. Catherine Walker and Dr. Katherine Uno for their important comments and guidance.

My research in India was made possible through a Junior Fellowship Award from the American Institute of Indian Studies. I wish to thank the staff of the American Institute of Indian Studies, Chicago and Delhi, for their support, and Dr. Kapil Kumar of Indira Gandhi University, Delhi, for his guidance while I was in India.

My research in London was partially supported by a grant from Temple University.

I wish to acknowledge the assistance given by the staff of the Indian National Archives, Delhi; Nehru Memorial Library and Museum, Delhi; Uttar Pradesh State Archives, Lucknow; and many other university libraries in Delhi. Thanks are also due to the staff of the India Office Library and the British Museum and Library, London; Temple University Library, Pennsylvania; and the Library of the University of Pennsylvania.

My deep appreciation is due to Mrs. Marianna Hashorva and to Mr. Frank Hashorva for their warm and sincere friendship and support throughout my studies. I also thank my many other friends.

I thank my family, Mr. Uday Pratap Singh, our son, in particular, for his patient technical assistance in the completion of this manuscript.

PREFACE

This study of women's experiences as victims and criminals in the North-Western Provinces and Oudh in colonial India lies at the intersection of several fields—colonial history, women's history, political economy, and the history of crime and punishment.

Its interdisciplinary approach permits it to argue that women's crime was largely induced by colonial intervention, oppression, and exploitation, and that punishment was used as a method of social control and repression. It shows that moral deviance was defined as crime in modern terms and that laws were passed to punish the guilty, but often women alone were left obeying such laws. Thus, while colonial intervention often reformulated and intensified older customs, it also invented newer practices extending women's oppression and exploitation to each aspect of its domination as the need arose. Consequently, the process of colonial state formation, the increasing number of women criminals during the last half of the nineteenth century, and imprisonment as a method to control deviance all proceeded at the same pace.

And while an alliance of British imperial interests and native patriarchy abused and exploited women in each place in society—domestic and religious circles, economic and political development, and judicial and penal systems—it was the ideology of low caste "immorality" and a lack of respectability that provided a justification to the rulers to use, abuse, and demoralize lower castes and classes of women as had not been done before. But by distorting history, colonial rulers established the moralizing and modernizing mission of the Raj while at the same time they demoralized the majority of women. It is this mainstream developmentalism within Indian studies which comes under the most severe scrutiny here.

More immediately, from the point of women victims and/or criminals, this study is historical and implies that it was the reaction of women to their oppression and violation that made them criminals; but it also stipulates that the boundary between a woman victim and/or criminal under those circumstances was often quite ambiguous. Therefore, their punishment often did not fit their crime. The fact that the law enforcement agencies and the justice and penal systems only re-victimized those very women is of tremendous significance, not only for Indian women and not only in women's history and studies, but also in the current ongoing debate in the United States about "battered women syndrome." Does a battered woman receive appropriate assistance from her family members, the law enforcement agencies, and the justice system? And is a woman who is battered and abused repeatedly over a period of time—whether physically, psychologically, emotionally, or financially—and who reacts violently under stress guilty of the crime she commits? This is of marked relevance to criminal and justice systems, for in crime and punishment, and in society's perception of a woman as a violator or as violated, the label of either "victim" or "criminal" is put upon her. This debate is only just beginning to be an important issue.

Abuse, oppression, violation, and exploitation of females come in many forms and from many quarters. And although the nature and intensity of crimes against women differ from one society to another, some crimes, such as rape and domestic violence, are common to many societies and they have continued with time.

The nature of the crimes women commit in reaction to their victimization—either under stress or in retaliation—also differs from one place to another. While the women victims, the forms of their reactions to violence and abuse, and the women criminals I deal with in this work are specific and historical, they are also contemporary and comparative.

Finally, although today the question of women in Indian society has taken a new form, recent studies show that oppression and victimization of the lower castes and classes of women and, of women generally, have not disappeared with India's independence and national rule. Such conclusions suggest that continuing influence of colonial culture must be taken into account in women's post-colonial history. Generations of habits, ideas, power relations, gender relations, and the superior/inferior complex did not disappear simply because India gained its freedom at a certain point in time. Therefore, I have suggested that women have continued to experience some of the legacies of the colonial rule and colonial culture in different forms even today.

INTRODUCTION

In a narrow sense, this is a study of women who became involved with the criminal justice system either as victims or offenders in the North-Western Provinces and Oudh[1] in colonial India. The study, in its broadest sense, analyzes at some length how women suffered disadvantages and abuse in each place in society; how through their reactions to their oppression and violence[2] they came to be criminals; how the justice system marginalized their interests; and how the penal system demoralized them and returned them to the society as an abandoned underclass.

I begin my analysis by noting that Hindu women's low and inferior position in society relative to men's position has often made them victims rather than perpetrators of crimes. Some well-known crimes and injustices against women include Sati (burning of widows on their husbands' pyre) during the first half of the nineteenth century; female infanticide, enforced widowhood, and child-marriages during the second half of the last century; and bride burning and female infanticide in our own time—though all have or had been confined to certain castes and classes only.

It is not surprising, therefore, that the nineteenth-century missionaries, travelers, and colonial administrators illustrated a generally "negative perception" of Hindu women.[3] In depicting their condition as pitiful and degraded, Western critics felt that Hindu religious customs were "imbued with immoralities and impurities." They saw the evils of Hindu ideas as the "consecration of immorality by the sanction of religion,"[4] which had actually debased not only certain castes and classes of females, but all Hindu women. Many Western philanthropists, such as Katherine Mayo, the well-known American journalist on India,[5] also followed the same line of rationalization and sensationalism in her writings on the connection between debased Hindu precepts and oppression of Hindu women. And to their own criticism of Indian culture, many of these writers found an answer in the "moralizing and civilizing mission" of the West.

Colonial history has itself interpreted colonial rule as one of modernizing and of improving the "moral" and "material" conditions of the natives. In such a system, criminality was interpreted as a symptom of deviance and criminal justice as a way to deal with criminals and deviants, in an increasingly rational social order. Such reasonings as the "unlimited faith" of the Indian peasant and the cultivator "in the authority and in the justice of British rule"[6] created a further need, or so it was explained, to "pursue and to punish" criminals for the protection of property and for "Society and Public Order."[7]

Other recent writers have followed the same line of rationalization to explain the position of Hindu-Indian women as static and sorrowful.[8] They claim that it was the coming of the West with its dynamic civilizing, moralizing, and modernizing mission that created profound changes for the better.

But what this line of reasoning has neglected to consider is that the most obvious paradox affecting the nineteenth-century Indian society was precisely that while progressive forces—in politics, philosophy, economy, and the judiciary system based on the Western model—were all being ushered in at a tremendous pace, ancient social institutions mostly affecting women were being preserved by the native patriarchy with help from the colonial government. One most obvious result of this incongruity was that Hindu women were caught between old Hindu customs and new colonial criminal laws. Women, indeed, experienced drastic changes under the colonial rule, but those changes were not always for the better nor were they for all women. Of the two distinct polarized classes created by the colonial policy—the small, upper, and "respectable," and a large, lower, and "immoral"—merely a handful of the upper strata of women enjoyed the Western "progress." For the others, destitution and demoralization were more the order of the times.[9]

The traditional view has also not questioned why the subaltern class of females was generally characterized as immoral by the colonial rulers. Moreover, it retains the theory that some people are "born criminals" and explains prostitution as a form of deviant behavior without analyzing how and why women came to be prostitutes.

Nor has this line of explanation analyzed satisfactorily the motivation behind the commonest crime, petty theft, when the overwhelming number of female (and male) prisoners in colonial jails were those who stole handfuls of grains to satisfy hunger. It interprets the cause of most petty thefts as desperate responses to seasonal crop failures without taking into consideration class relations and class conflict, expanding capitalism, cultivation of cash crops, export of food grains, and consequent high prices of grains—all of which helped to exacerbate scarcities, famines, hunger, and crimes.

This traditional line of colonial historiography has been challenged by many recent historians and social scientists.[10] They have shown that in various societies the modern transformation of culture and political economy can be understood as a reactive process between, on the one hand, power and domination and, on the other, a social complex of resistance and disorder. They have also demonstrated that criminal justice under "modernization" appears as a method of social control and repression.

At the same time, other researchers have explored crime as a feature of colonial India. They have shown how "British definitions of crime in India were related to the larger ideas about the structure and the functioning of Indian society and culture as well as to the ideology of rule which justified British domination and Indian subjugation."[11] Focusing on authority and criminal law, it has been contended that "moral influence" was fused with the concept of the "power of state" to guard against "collective crimes" that the state deemed a direct threat to its authority. But the colonial authorities gave far less attention to the individual crime.[12] Research has also shown that the colonial justice system was, more often than not, another tool of oppression of the poor and the weak.

From the point of view of women's history, other scholars have made women and gender relations an important, creative component in their examinations of colonial India. It has been shown that now in the post-independence capitalist development, women subsistence producers are providing "hidden work" for their own survival as well as for "capital accumulation."[13] My research shows that this process was true of the colonial period as well. On the other hand, others have argued that "both tradition and modernity have been, in India, carriers of patriarchal ideologies." And "both tradition and modernity are eminently colonial constructs."[14] Concentrating on gender relations, they have illustrated how the collusion between pre-colonial patriarchal norms and the colonial state actually "invented" traditions that did not help the women's cause.[15]

My work differs somewhat from the above scholars in that I have used political and socioeconomic changes and crime[16] as a framework to explore women's experiences as victims and criminals in colonial state formation.[17] And in contradiction to the modernizationist view, I have used political economic theory to analyze women's position in a colonial historical context. This line of inquiry—which seeks to explain changes in the politics and economics of class relations—has a broader conception of imperialism,[18] and it is better suited to explain how the process of colonial hegemony in the nineteenth century transformed different aspects of subjugated societies. It thus widens the meaning of class consciousness, class relationship, gender relations, class conflict, and history. The social structure implied here is one composed of the ruled and the ruler, the powerful and the powerless.

However, to study and explain women and their crime, I have broadened the concepts that will analyze their specific experiences, both as victims and criminals. For such a study, the conceptualization of state formation as an ongoing process, rather than as something "formed" and "unchanging," helps us to understand how the changing process of the state transformed, as well, the structure of the society under its domination; how changing resultant socioeconomic situations created crimes and criminals; and how the Raj (as the British rule is referred to in India), in reference to such changes, formulated laws to define crime as well as punishment, all as an ongoing process. And since state formation and victimization/criminalization of females were not determined by economics alone, this perspective allows us to explain how the changing political imperatives over a period of time impelled the developing state to make decisions not only in economics, but in social, domestic, religious, political, and juridical systems that actually affected women and men most vulnerable within each domain.

Since the intrusion of an alien culture into villages, through different agents of the State, had a profound impact on village life and rural women, the effects of such an impact have also been explored here to show how those agents changed village traditions and, in particular, the family structure. The weakening of family structure, on the one hand, and the reformulation of patriarchy to control women, on the other, might explain many types of crime against women—among them, the murder of unknown or unidentified women—often reported during that period in vernacular papers.

And finally, this approach to the study of women's crime and punishment has also taken into account both "inter and intra class relationship, gender relations, the different aspects of the family including generational and gender differences, as well as the changing role of the family itself in transforming history."[19]

A definition of crime, however, which encompasses all its different aspects, or which fulfills the need to describe every offense, is practically impossible to create. Therefore, crime for the purpose of this study is simply defined as an "illegal behaviour which, if detected and prosecuted, leads to a criminal charge answerable in a court of law, and carrying certain penalties."[20] And, while some pioneering theoretical guidelines for the study of crime have been established,[21] the study of women criminals in colonial India, nonetheless, remains a new field. Thus, there is a marked gap between theory and fact in the study of the effects of British colonial rule on Indian women.

One drawback to the use of crime in the colonial period as a major source is the inability of the researcher to compare women's crime with crime in the pre-colonial period. Even if records were available of the pre-colonial period, which they are not, a comparison of crime and punishment of the two periods would be practically impossible because of the marked difference between Hindu/Muslim and the British Criminal Justice and Penal Laws.[22] The definition of deviancies in legal criminal terms, the institution of law enforcement agencies to detect and to report crimes, and the penal system, as we know the juridical system in India today, were all new innovations under the Raj.[23] The gradual emergence of criminal legal laws began in the North-Western Provinces early in the nineteenth century under the East India Company, but the establishment of a uniform system of legal laws and rights was not achieved until the post-Mutiny period under the imperial rule.[24]

An analysis of the majority of women's conditions in the North-Western Provinces and Oudh, however, does reveal that their experience as victims and criminals under colonial rule was very different from that of their male counterparts. Therefore, while such theories of "collective social protest" might explain some crimes committed by men, as opposed to "real" deviant behavior, they do not explain female victim cum criminal in nineteenth-century India, those women who were invariably found guilty of their crimes, punished, and easily ignored. This study focuses on that large majority of women even though records do show occasional cases of actual deviant behavior in women. One Mussammat (Miss/Mrs.) Madhea, for instance, was convicted and sentenced to eight years of rigorous imprisonment following the attempted murder of her brother-in-law.[25] Another case involved a young wife, fourteen years old, who was involved in the murder of her husband. Apparently, she kept her lover concealed in the bedroom and had him murder her husband with an ax while the husband was asleep.[26] What is not known in this case, though, is whether the fourteen-year-old woman was simply implicated in the murder by the murderer or by her family itself, as was known to happen. In another case, a jealous woman, after a quarrel with her blind lover, killed him with a hatchet and buried him under the floor. The smell of the decomposed body led to the discovery of the crime.[27] Of course, the specific dakait-related (dakait or dacoit is plunder and robbery, often accompanied by murder and rape) activities of female criminal tribes who robbed others to feed their own poor can be explained as an example of a "Robin Hood" type of crime.

One obstacle to discussing Indian/Hindu women under colonialism, and even under today's social system, however, must also be noted. There were, and are, numerous variations in the characteristics of the Indian society. Religion, religious ideology, customs, caste/class/sociocultural attitudes and values, gender relations, family structure, economic environment, and social and economic standing frequently dictated a woman's position in the family and in society. And those same factors, and caste/class relations in particular, also determined the nature of her oppression and her crime. Therefore, making broad assertions about Indian women's condition and position in society at any given time and space without censuring some specific customs is practically impossible.

Consequently, rather than focusing on Indian society as a whole, I have concentrated on Hindu women. They not only represented the majority of the population, but such customary practices as Sati, female infanticide, child-marriage, and enforced widowhood (all particularly applied to high-caste women), which generated the most criticism, were Hindu customs and affected Hindu women. But it is not implied here that Muslim, native Christian, and English females did not commit crimes. They did, as the jail records show (see Appendix B). They all committed crimes in proportion to their numbers and because of their respective circumstances. And they also suffered the consequences of colonialism, but the focus here is on Hindu women.

Nor have I used the rural/urban comparative method in this study. One reason is that, of the total population of 44,107,869 in the North-Western Provinces and Oudh in 1881, for instance, 90.3 percent of the people lived in rural areas.[28] Consequently, most villages contained their generally high-caste/class rich and the low-caste/class poor.

The other pertinent point to be noted in regard to Hindu women is that it was the high-caste Hindu woman who was the central figure in nineteenth-century India. It was she who was debased by missionaries and Western writers, and it was she who was regenerated by the nationalist reformers. The other lower castes and classes of women, as Uma Chakravarti has observed, "did not exist for the nineteenth century nationalists."[29] In fact, it would not be inappropriate to say that the social condition and abuse of a large majority of the lower caste/class women (and men) under colonialism were ignored by the higher caste/middle-class Indian society. And perhaps because theirs was an "unacknowledged existence," the paucity of information available on this subaltern class is not surprising. Their history, which is often derogatory in nature, has to be pieced together from bits of scattered information from different sources.

The caste system, which is also important in the study of Hindu society, is for our purposes based on the simple five-layered caste structure: Brahman (priests), Kshatriya (rulers/warriors), Vaishya (traders), Sudra (various classes of artisans), and Harijans (untouchables).[30] In general, the highest castes/classes were also the richest landowning class. Various shades of middle classes were also generally of the higher castes. They were smaller landowners, moneylenders, the educated class of bureaucrats, and the like; hence, their designation as high-caste/middle-class in this study. The lower castes/classes came from the large majority of the lower ranks of Sudras and the Harijans. They were the poor landless class of laborers. However, there were some high-caste groups who were also poor and landless. They were, therefore, high-caste but economically low-class groups (high-caste/low-class). Thus, while caste distinction remained constant, classes, to some extent, shaded from one level into the next.[31]

There were also various distinctions between high-caste/middle-class and low-caste/low-class domestic lives. Middle-class homes were generally composed of extended families where sanctity and seclusion of females were observed.[32] Their women were subject to stringent religious and social customs (such as enforced widowhood, where widows were not permitted to remarry on religious grounds) and patriarchal norms. While they had economic security, their oppression within domestic circles was not unknown. And their suicides, because of domestic violence,[33] and their "immoralities" and crimes associated with enforced widowhood, as evidenced by jail records, were also not uncommon.

The low-caste/class homes were based on nuclear families,[34] with females under patriarchal domination. And because of their low economic condition, they participated in the rural economy for subsistence.[35] However, because of their lowest caste and class position in society, they suffered exploitation and social abuse in their economic, domestic, and civilian lives.

Keeping in focus the particular variations that applied to Indian/Hindu societies, I have chosen a multifaceted but ultimately more holistic approach—one that investigates women's position in every aspect of colonial hegemony. It is contended that a combination of factors led to the exploitation, oppression, and victimization of women as colonial domination progressed. And in the majority of the cases studied, it was the reaction of the women to their oppression/victimization that led them into different forms of criminality. The line between a female victim and a female criminal, therefore, was often not clear.

Chapter 1 explores the close link between economic changes, pauperization, and women's criminality. I also examine how changes in politics and economics of the provinces created a new structure of class relations, and how peasant oppression and extraction of peasant surplus by landlords and moneylenders kept peasants in perpetual destitution. It is asserted here that it was peasant indebtedness and pauperization, more than famines, that created scarcities, poverty, and crimes.

Another factor that contributed to peasant poverty was the commercialization of agriculture. Some British officials looked upon the Indian method of agriculture as a "barbarity of the old world,"[36] and they, representatives of the modern Western world, sought to modernize peasant agriculture as well. Questions that have been explored include: What effect did modernization of agriculture have on peasants? Who gained from increasing market economy? What were the causes and effects of the disintegration of the traditional village system; how did these new conditions affect women; and what were their consequent crimes and their punishments?

Emigration was also a part of the same complex and changing conditions. Was it encouraged by the State to relieve overpopulation? How did it affect women? Very little research has been done to analyze the total consequences of the nineteenth-century migration in the provinces. Maria Mies[37] has, however, found that one of the consequences of the current capitalist expansion in India and its related poverty is the migration to urban areas of male peasants in search of employment. They leave their wives and children behind. This economic migration not only breaks up the traditional family, but also leaves women alone to find alternative means of support. Unfortunately, they often turn to crime. This process of migration analyzed by Maria Mies, in fact, began under the colonial rule.

In Chapter 2, by exploring the experiences of two specific groups of females—women in domestic circles and widows—it has been shown that the interaction of colonial rule and the native patriarchy led to the subjugation and oppression of most castes and classes of women. This chapter explores what prompted the interaction of colonial and native patriarchal[38] interests; how it stratified gender relations; how women's crimes of suicide and murder-suicide were related to their domestic lives; and how the colonial law punished these women.

An analysis of the condition of widows further suggests that there is a need to go beyond a discourse of Sati. The current area of inquiry, such as that of Lata Mani, V. N. Datta, and others,[39] is to see whether or not Sati was intensified because of the intrusion of an alien culture into the Hindu society. This line of inquiry has been extended to see how, following the abolition of Sati, the prolonged controversy on widow-remarriage and child-marriages contributed to the making of twenty-five million widows in the country around the turn of the century; how the issue of enforced widowhood became a part of religious ideology; how it was linked to women's crimes; and why the colonial government was unable to legislate against child-marriages and enforced widowhood with effective legislation.[40]

Under the heading of state and women, this study contends that the colonial state's glaring abuse of women was nowhere better illustrated than in the case of lower castes/classes of peasant women. Chapter 3 examines how the process of state hegemony progressed and how its policies in three areas—the establishment of army cantonments in village India; the cultivation, manufacture, and sale of drugs and liquor; and the emigration policy—affected and disrupted village lives with particular attention to their effects on women. Grafted upon the Hindu system of caste relations was an ideology of "morality/respectability." Why was this ideology used to divide and polarize women into higher castes/classes with high morals and respectability, and lower castes/classes with "immoral" traits and lack of respectability? How did this ideology affect the lower castes/classes of women? These are pertinent but long-ignored issues that lead us to a clearer understanding of the many-sided effects of the colonial rule.

In Chapter 4, the line of inquiry is extended to the experiences of women in the developing colonial justice system. What were the experiences of the accused women as they faced the judicial, criminal, and penal systems? What were the experiences of women convicts in the provincial prisons as well as in the penal colonies of the Andamans and the Nicobar Islands? A study of the transportation (transportation, as used in the jail records, meant deportation of convicts to the penal colonies) of female convicts reveals how women were once again exploited because of their gender. Their transportation orders came not because women prisoners formed a dangerous class, but because there was a need for them to serve the political imperatives of the colonial state. What this chapter shows is how the majority of the female ex-convicts, who were sexually exploited and thoroughly debauched by the "reform-minded" penal system, became an underclass of ostracized women.

Two more issues pertaining to this work need to be explained. One is the focus on the area of the study, the North-Western Provinces and Oudh, and the other is the approximate time frame, 1870–1910.

The second half of the nineteenth century was important in many respects, as was my choice of region. Colonial state formation, which is defined here as a continuous and ongoing process, began in 1858 upon the transfer of ruling power from the East India Company to the Imperial Government following the Mutiny of 1857. And with it came many political, economic, and social changes in the provinces. In agricultural development, as Elizabeth Whitcombe has noted, numerous and rapid economic changes under imperial rule were witnessed. "The North-Western Provinces and Oudh were drawn by their very geography into the forefront of the grand design" of development for "a generous as well as rapid return."[41] Land settlement (as in Oudh), the process of class formation, and their interrelated economic changes also began as a part of the political economy of the state formation during these initial stages of the imperial rule.[42] And this period was also marked with famines and famine-like conditions, poverty, and crime, with a corresponding increase in the jail population.

From the point of view of women's history more specifically, the period was characterized by such issues as child-marriage, widow-remarriage, and Western criticism of Hindu women's low status in society and of their general oppression. In reaction to Western criticism, the middle-class nationalist reformers also created a new image of middle-class womanhood in contradiction to Western women, on the one hand, and the lower caste/class Indian women, on the other.[43] In the process, these reformers not only neglected the lower caste/class woman, they also subjugated the middle-class woman to "a new patriarchy."[44]

In the area of law enforcement, again a point in women's history, the Indian Penal Code was instituted in this period as the law of the land (1860), and the Code of Criminal Procedure was instituted in 1861.[45]

The termination date for this study, the first decade of the twentieth century, was chosen because, with the issues of the independence movement and World War I, although many of the older problems continued, the question of women's position in Indian history entered a new phase.

Another important topic that needs to be mentioned is that of the sources. An effort was made to use a wide variety of sources from many archives and libraries. Because this study is multidisciplinary, holistic, and in part theoretical, the choice of sources is quite varied. No one is decisive or stands alone. I use works of reflection by participants in my period and the later commentators on them. Those provide me with information and ideology. I use archival information largely from India about women and the criminal system. The subject of the female criminal is still a fairly new one. Archival information—with its inevitable gap—provides fascinating vignettes of particular crimes along with some statistics. One cannot, of course, interpret something in terms of itself. Thus, I interpret what I find in light of the prevailing works on social history, political economy, and feminist history which bears on my period.

One major drawback, however, has been the lack of sources reflecting women's own authentic viewpoint. It also seems that much information on criminal cases was lost during the annual official "weeding" out and in the destruction and rearrangement process of criminal records during the period under this study.[46] Therefore, most published sources of criminal information and criminal statistics have been drawn from police records and jail records. Though they might be inaccurate and inconsistent, they nonetheless remain a valuable and uniquely informative source. Other official records, official publications, court cases where available, settlement reports, press accounts, journals, and books have all been used for information.

I have intended this study to be an exploration of women's as-yet-neglected history in the colonial state formation. I wanted to contribute to the literature showing that colonial policies and the interaction of the colonial state and the native patriarchy have had profound effects upon women's lives. My examination of the use by the state of religion, morality/immorality, caste/class, gender and sex relations, and other policies to exploit, oppress, and criminalize women reveals the variety of women's suffering under the colonial rule. And most important, what we finally see is that women's reactions to certain forms of oppression provide our best understanding of the more specific topic here—the nature and causes of their crimes.

Criminals are individual women. Inevitably, one must be aware of the points of tension that emerge using the transformation of the economy and society and the crimes to which these appear to give rise as correlates.[47] There is subjectivity and individual specificity, as the archival cases reveal.

NOTES

1. In 1881, the North-Western Provinces and Oudh contained forty-nine districts with an area of 105,603 square miles. Its population ran a close second to Bengal with 44,107,669 inhabitants, and exceeded that of England and Wales together or of France. The provinces were comprised of something like 106,200 villages and several large towns. The population was about 85 percent Hinds, 14 percent Muslim, and 1 percent all other religions. For the detection and repression of crime, 32,000 officers, constables, and chaukidars (village watchmen) were employed.
   Oudh was administered separately until February 1877, when the Offices—the Commissioner of Oudh and Lieutenant-Governor of the North-Western Provinces—were united. The provinces were named the United Provinces of Agra and Oudh in 1902. *Police Administration, Police Reports of North-Western Provinces and Oudh for 1881*, no. 1522A of 1882 (Allahabad: Government Press, 1882), p. 2 (hereafter cited as Police Reports). After the independence, the provinces were renamed Uttar Pradesh. Shiva S. Dua, *Society and Culture in Northern India, 1850–1910* (New Delhi: Indian Bibliographies Bureau Co-Publisher, 1985), p. 6.
2. The terms "victimized," "abused," "exploited," "degraded," and "oppressed," as used in this study, define malpractices that were generally applied consistently against those who occupied the weakest social positions, were powerless, economically dependent, and who seldom had any social or legal recourse against their perpetrators.
3. Cecil H. Walsh, *Indian Village Crimes* (London: Ernest Benn, 1929), p. 20; "The Women of India," *The Calcutta Review*, 36 (January–June 1861): 315–343; and Bishop Henry Whitehead, in a letter written to Katherine Mayo, quoted in Katherine Mayo, *Slaves of the Gods* (New York: Harcourt, Brace & Co., 1929), p. 7.
4. For instance, Bishop Henry Whitehead, ibid.
5. Katherine Mayo, *Mother India* (New York: Blue Ribbon Books, 1927); and *Slaves of the Gods*.
6. Cecil H. Walsh, *Crime in India with an Introduction on Forensic Difficulties and Peculiarities* (London: Ernest Benn, 1933), "Introduction," p. 11.
7. Ibid.
8. Mrs. H. Gray, "The Progress of Women," *Modern India and the West: A Study of the Interaction of Their Civilizations*, L. S. S. O'Malley, ed. (London: Oxford University Press, 1941), pp. 45, 483.
9. Dua, *Society and Culture*, p. 151; O'Malley, ed., *Modern India and the West*, pp. 128–137; James Samuelson, *India, Past and Present: Historical, Social, and Political* (London: Trubner & Co., 1890); and Reverend John Morrison, *New Ideas in India during the Nineteenth Century: A Study of Social, Political, and Religious Developments* (Chandigarh: Sameer Prakashan, 1977), pp. 4, 5.
10. Such as Ranajit Guha and the Subaltern School.
11. Such as David Arnold and various contributors to *Crime and Criminality in British India*, Anand Yang, ed. (Tucson: University of Arizona Press, 1985); quote from "Introduction," p. 13.

12 ■ INTRODUCTION

12. Sandria Freitag, "Collective Crime and Authority in North India," in Yang, ed., *Crime and Criminality*, p. 16.
13. Maria Mies, *The Lace Makers of Narsapur: Indian Housewives Produce for the World Market* (London: Zed Books, 1982), pp. 4, 5.
14. Kumkum Sangari and Sudesh Vaid, eds., *Recasting Women: Essays in Colonial India* (New Delhi: Kali for Women, 1989), "Introduction," p. 17.
15. Ibid.
16. The disadvantages in the study of crime, such as offenses not reported or cases not prosecuted though reported, as Siddique points out, give an incomplete picture of the actual crimes committed. Further, the largely hidden information about sexual crimes, illegitimate infanticide, and domestic violence creates inherent deficiencies of the statistics of criminal behavior (Ahmed Siddique, *Criminology: Problems and Perspectives* [Lucknow: Eastern Book Co., 1977], p. 7).
17. Christine Ward Gailey, *Kinship to Kingship: Gender Hierarchy and State Formation in the Tongan Islands* (Austin: University of Texas Press, 1987), "Introduction," p. ix. I have adopted and used in this work Gailey's conceptualization of state formation as a continuous and ongoing process.
18. Peter Gran, "Paradigms for the Study of the Middle East," seminar paper presented at Temple University, History Department, fall semester, 1988.
19. Patricia O'Brien, "Crime and Punishment as Historical Problem," *Journal of Social History*, vol. 11, no. 4 (1978): 515.
20. J. A. Sharpe, "The History of Crime in Late Medieval and Early Modern England: A Review of the Field," *Social History*, vol. 7, no. 2 (1982): 188.
21. Michel Foucault, Patricia O'Brien, J. A. Sharpe, J. M. Beattie, Robert Nye, E. P. Thompson, Douglas Hay, and Peter Linebaugh.
22. H. R. Fink, "Crimes and Punishments under Hindu Law," *The Calcutta Review*, vol. 61 (1875): 123–141.
23. H. R. Fink, "Crimes and Punishments"; Sharpe, "The History of Crime," p. 188; Yogendra Singh, *Modernization of Indian Tradition: A Systematic Study of Social Change* (Delhi: Thomson Press India Ltd., 1973), p. 96; Dharma Bhanu, *History and Administration of the North-Western Provinces, 1803–1858* (subsequently called the Agra Province) (Agra: Shiva Lal Agarwala & Co. Private Ltd., 1955), pp. 220–259; and Benjamin Lindsay, "Law," in *Modern India and the West*, O'Malley, ed., chap. 3.
24. Ibid. (Fink, Singh, Dharma Bhanu, and Lindsay).
25. *The Pioneer*, April 10, 1890, p. 4.
26. Ibid., July 5, 1890, p. 4.
27. Ibid., October 1, 1890, p. 2.
28. *Census of 1881*. The Indian Empire. Report. Abstract No. LXXXll, vol. 1 (London: Eyre and Spottiswoode, 1883), p. 272. Most castes/classes and religious groups lived separately in their own designated areas in villages.
29. Uma Chakravarti, "Whatever Happened to the Vedic Dasi? Orientalism, Nationalism, and a Script for the Past," in Sangari and Vaid, eds., *Recasting Women*, p. 79.
30. M. N. Srinivas, *The Remembered Village* (Berkeley, Los Angeles, and London: University of California Press, 1980), pp. 169, 170.
31. Ibid.
32. Dua, *Society and Culture*; and Samuelson, *India, Past and Present*, p. 59.
33. "The Women of India," pp. 315–343.

34. Dua, *Society and Culture*, p. 150; and Samuelson, *India, Past and Present*, p. 59.
35. Subsistence here is defined as economy for daily survival (Mies, *The Lace Makers of Narsapur*, p. 3).
36. C. W. McMinn, *Famine Truths, Half Truths, and Untruths* (London, 1902), p. 192; quoted in Elizabeth Whitcombe, *Agrarian Conditions in Northern India: The United Provinces under British Rule, 1860–1900*, vol. 1 (Berkeley, Los Angeles, and London: University of California Press, 1972), p. 99.
37. Maria Mies, "Capitalist Development and Subsistence Production: Rural Women in India," in *Women: The Last Colony*, Maria Mies, Veronika Bennholdt-Thomsen, and Claudia Von Werlhof, eds. (London: Zed Books, 1988) p. 42.
38. There is disagreement on the theory of "patriarchy": The issue is whether an exclusively gender-based approach can in general explain social reality since there were women who had control over the mode of production; for instance, there were women landholders and moneylenders in the region under this study (Kapil Kumar, "Rural Women in Oudh, 1917–47: Baba Ram Chandra and the Women's Question," in Sangari and Vaid, eds., *Recasting Women*, p. 335).

However, since that class of women was also largely denied social/political power and was bound by social customs and patriarchy, the word "patriarchy," for the purpose of this study of the nineteenth-century family structure in the North-Western Provinces and Oudh, is defined as a system of male domination and female subordination in economy, politics, and/or society and culture.
39. Lata Mani, "Contentious Traditions: The Debate on Sati in Colonial India," in Sangari and Vaid, eds., *Recasting Women*, p. 88; and V. N. Datta, *Sati: Widow Burning in India* (New Delhi: Manohar Publications, 1988).
40. The aim here is to show how women were affected by the government's decision to refrain from passing effective laws. Whether the colonial "government established by law in British India," as claimed by the rulers (quoted by Iqbal Singh in *The Andaman Story* [Delhi: Vikas Publishing House Pvt. Ltd., 1978], p. 189), that was "moralizing" and "modernizing" the natives should have intervened in the interests of the colonized native women (the answer to that would depend on one's viewpoint) is not the sole issue. Nevertheless, in 1861, *The Calcutta Review* reported that women of India outnumbered the entire population of Great Britain, France, and Italy; and that "any custom and law, therefore, that affected their well-being, affected a considerable portion of the human population" (*The Calcutta Review*, vol. 36 [January–June 1861]: 315.
41. Whitcombe, Agrarian Conditions, "Preface," p. x.
42. Kapil Kumar, *Peasants in Revolt: Tenants, Landlords, Congress, and the Raj in Oudh, 1886–1922* (New Delhi: Manohar Publications, 1984), p. 14.
43. Partha Chatterjee, "Colonialism, Nationalism, and Colonized Women: The Contest in India, the Woman's Question in Tradition," *American Ethnologist*, vol. 16, no. 4 (1989): 622–633; and Chakravarti, "Whatever Happened to the Vedic Dasi?" pp. 27–87.
44. Pratha Chatterjee, "The Nationalist Resolution of the Women's Question," in Sangari and Vaid, eds., *Recasting Women*, pp. 244, 245.
45. Dua, *Society and Culture*, p. 151.
46. *Oudh Administration, (Criminal) Justice Reports for 1890*, no. 1760 (Lucknow:

Printed by the Oudh Government, 1891), p. 177 (hereafter cited as *Oudh Administration Reports*); and *Oudh Criminal Courts, Judicial (Criminal) Department, Proceedings on the Destruction of Records* [January 1901], file no. 484C.
47. David Jones, *Crime, Protest, Community, and Police in Nineteenth-Century Britain* (London and Boston: Routledge & Kegan Paul, 1982), p. 31.

1

Economic Deprivation and Women's Criminality

The jail report of the North-Western Provinces and Oudh for 1895 reads, "It will be observed that the increase in the number of female prisoners during the year was very marked, viz., 4,033 against 2,922 in 1894."[1] The reports for the years 1896 and 1897 were, however, far worse when the figures recorded were 7,233 and 9,639, respectively.[2]

The common female crimes listed were as follows:

1. House-breaking and house-trespass
2. Theft in building
3. Receiving stolen property
4. Attempt to commit suicide
5. Mischief
6. Kidnapping, abduction, and selling minors into slavery
7. Causing miscarriage and exposing children
8. Murder and attempt to murder[3]

The jail records of the provinces further established the first four crimes as economic related caused by poverty, but poverty was said to be linked to recurrent scarcities and famines. The other serious crimes—suicides, kidnappings, abductions, and murders—though also frequently entered in the reports, either could not be explained by harassed officials, or were explained as the result of some sort of "native traits."

It is true that scarcities, famines, and poverty caused crimes, as the jail record of 1877 had established: "Influx of prisoners, consequent on the prevalent privation and distress brought up the jail population of the year."[4] Thirty-two years later, in 1909, it was still being reported that poverty and "indebtedness [was] no doubt very great," since it had been reported right through the period.[5] Tables 1 and 2 show the influx of female criminals in the provincial jails.

What these jail statistics illustrate is that there was a dramatic rise in the female jail population during the famine years of 1877–1888 and

1896–1897; and there was also an increase in their number during the scarcities of 1880 and 1891–1892. But even if these years of famines and scarcities are eliminated, there was a consistent rise in the number of female jail inmates all through the 1870s to the 1890s in absolute terms and relative to men. There was then a sharp decline in their number after the turn of the century.

Contrary to the official explanation that crimes followed the failure of rains and loss of crops, or that crimes were the result of some sort of native traits, the first section of this chapter illustrates that scarcities and famines, in fact, resulted partly from the deliberate political and socioeconomic decisions made by the Imperial Government.[6] Continuous peasant-indebtedness and destitution; their inability to pay rents and consequent evictions from their lands; excessive rates in death; and emigration of male laborers abroad were all elements in a chain reaction to the same political economy, as were the increasing rates in crime and prison population. Nor did the commercialization of agriculture help the peasants; it in fact, added to their hardship.

TABLE 1: Total Female Prisoners at the End of the Year in the Jails of the North-Western Provinces and Oudh between 1876 and 1909[7]

Year	Number of Female Convicts	Year	Number of Female Convicts	Year	Number of Female Convicts
1876	5,037	1888	6,180	1900	2,992
1877	5,929*	1889	6,948	1901	2,224
1878	11,043*	1890	7,091	1902	1,905
1879	1,588	1891	8,335**	1903	1,830
1880	5,497**	1892	6,883**	1904	1,586
1881	5,120	1893	6,240	1905	1,872
1882	4,796	1894	8,575	1906	1,809
1883	2,803	1895	8,617	1907	1,576**
1884	2,803	1896	8,663*	1908*	1,761**
1885	5,409	1897	11,133*	1909*	1,536
1886	5,833	1898	4,878		
1887	5,915	1899	3,597*		

*Years of famines
**Years of scarcities

ECONOMIC DEPRIVATION AND CRIMINALITY

TABLE 2: Total Free Female Population of the Provinces and the Influx of Female Prisoners in the Jails between 1876 and 1911[8]

Year	Total Female Population in the Provinces	Prisoners at the Beginning of the Year	Prisoners Received during the Year	Total Daily Average	Remaining at the End of the Year
1876	20,060,127	1,573	6,437	1,443	1,514
1877*		1,516	7,898	1,448	1,845
1878*		1,574	11,043	2,216	2,070*
1880**					
1881	21,566,277				
1885		1,017	4,392	997	955
1886		955	4,878	993	938
1887		938	4,977	752	896
1888		896	5,284	974	1,005
1889		1,005	5,943	1,084	1,063
1890		1,063	6,038	1,074	1,139
1891**	22,977,789	1,139	7,196	1,251	1,234
1892**		1,234	5,649	1,180	1,097
1893		1,098	5,142	1,037	993
1894		993	5,582	1,086	1,179
1895		1,179	7,438	1,382	1,441
1896*		1,436	7,233	1,381	1,494
1897*		1,494	9,639	1,427	1,275
1898			4,878		
1899**					
1900					
1901	23,454,768				
1902			2,224		
1903		910	3,693	640	773
1904		773	3,180	716	666
1905		666	3,628	729	736
1906		671	1,809	719	698
1907		698	1,576	680	670
1908*		670	1,761	722	653
1909*		653	1,536	655	650
1910		650	1,429	658	604
1911	22,933,350				

*Famines
**Scarcities

The second section analyzes the effects of economic distress on women; their abandonment by their husbands; their crimes, and their punishment. They were all interrelated and were largely manifestations of the same political economy of the colonial rule. The increased jail population of impoverished peasants during the last half of the nineteenth century, was ultimately also a colonial creation designed to control deviancy in a modernizing and moralizing society.

Political Economy of the Imperial Government

The conscious decision of the rulers to change the interrelated political and socioeconomic relations that began with the imperial state formation after the Mutiny in 1858, was obvious from the following correspondence in the case of Oudh: "The Talookdars (revenue collectors) have both power and influence to exercise either for or against us. The village proprietors have neither."[9]

The most immediate outcome of that deliberation was the creation of a new landlord class; of men who were revenue collectors under the Mughal rule and who still wielded some power and influence to provide support to the developing colonial state.[10] That also meant the peasants—the actual occupants of the land who had neither "power" nor "influence" to serve the interests of the Raj—were all at once converted into tenants of the new landlords. The result of the new economic and social transformation heralded in by the Imperial Government to serve its political imperatives was manifold and had far-reaching consequences.

As expected, the new landlords facilitated the collection of land-revenue, "the maximum amount with a minimum expenditure."[11] The political imperatives—the need to create a class that would "exercise influence" in the interests of the rulers and also serve as a buffer between the masses and the rulers—were also realized. And, just as the rulers came to depend on the new landlord class to serve its interests, so too, the new landlord class came to rely on the rulers to support its position and status against peasants. Finally, by making this influential group of men into a landlord class and an ally, the rulers also eliminated any unforeseen threat to their rule from this powerful group of men.

But for the peasant, the alliance of the rulers, the new landlord, and the moneylender, who was often the landlord himself or the Bania (trader/moneylender caste), meant his "increasing domination,"[12] an unmerciful exploitation and extraction of his surplus,[13] which kept him in destitution. The empowering of the new landlords with such colonial legal laws as "The Court shall in no case enquire into the propriety of the rate of rent payable by a tenant, a tenant not having a right of occupancy . . . such amount as may be agreed upon between him and the landlord," [14] permitted them to enhance rents and to evict tenants at will when they failed to pay.[15]

Various methods devised to enhance land rents increased peasant indebtedness. Rents were determined by competition, that is, whoever paid the highest rent received the land;[16] threat of evictions was used as a form of coercion to enhance rent; and the practices of taking an "extra premium on rent" by instituting gift payments and levying extra taxes were applied regularly.

Nor did the colonial government's fixed revenue system help the peasants.[17] The concept of flexibility prior to the British rule, whereby, revenue was adjusted depending on local situations, no longer applied.[18] Now, even when the crops failed, the peasants had no relief from taxes. A conflict between a harvest calendar and a fiscal calendar further obliged the peasant to take loans for taxes during a period when the interest rates were exceptionally high; that also increased his economic distress.[19] Again, while the British revenue system created a need to borrow, it neither provided any credit system, rent laws, nor any enforceable ceiling on local interest rates to protect the peasant.[20]

The first result of peasant exploitation was that he with his meager earnings suffered perpetual indebtedness and destitution,[21] and for him and his family, a state of semi-starvation became a regular way of life.

The second result of high rents and high interest rates on loans was numerous evictions.[22] Eviction of peasants under Hindu law was not a practice, unless one was known to be of an undesirable character,[23] but under colonial power, evictions became a regular practice. And women generally, but widows in particular, became a systematic target of evictions from their landholdings and often with violence. The moneylenders, the landlords, and their agents deliberately oppressed them, charged exorbitant interest rates, forcefully withheld advanced money,[24] and evicted them even when their rents were paid.[25] Outright murders of women for their property[26] was not uncommon either.

But generally, evictions and threats of eviction became a source of peasant hardship. In Oudh, for example, during the years 1869–1889, 226,820 notices of eviction were issued.[27] And between 1880 and 1884, of the total number of tenants, 66,847, or 29 percent, were actually evicted.[28] In the North-Western Provinces and Oudh as a whole, the number of suits for evictions in 1905 was 74,264, and evictions were actually ordered in 63,022 cases.[29]

There were times when in desperation to pay rents so as to hold on to the lands, families sold their daughters and often to much older men perhaps because they could afford to buy them. The following shows the sale and the ages of girls by some peasants:

- A girl of five was sold by her brother to a husband of forty for 300 rupees.
- A girl of twelve was sold by her father to a husband of sixty for 330 rupees.
- A girl of seven was sold by her father to a husband of fifty for 200 rupees.
- A girl of twelve was sold by her father to a husband of thirty for 300 rupees.
- A girl of five was sold by her father to a husband of forty for 300 rupees.[30]

Although it was customary among certain classes to marry young girls to older men, the great age discrepancy in the above cases appears not to have been a general practice. Such accounts lead one to the conclusion that, in many cases, women and girls were the first victims of class changes and economic distress.

The problem with eviction also was that with each eviction of the head of the family, every member of the family lost his/her means of subsistence. What happened to these families who were evicted? Where did they go? Did they resort to crimes?

It seems that some retained their dwellings and garden plots and became semi-proletarianized.[31] Little is known of the others, except in one instance when in 1875 in Rae Bareli Division, "of the 3,087 cases of evictions who lost their entire holdings, 538 left their villages, 176 were reduced to idleness, and a few to beggary."[32] The Chief Commissioner of Rae Bareli, however, found no linkages between evictions and crime even when the jail population was on the rise. He noted that "those turned adrift from the land would not turn to organized crime."[33] But "organized crime" and individual crime because of hunger were not the same. In fact, in 1920, forty-five years later concerning the same continuing problem, Mehta in his report concluded that some landless became homeless, destitute, and "vagabonds."[34] The possession of land by the peasantry had, in fact, meant much more than a livelihood. It had given them a home, family, stability, and respectability. But those who lost their land completely tended to become lawless.[35]

Peasant exploitation, indebtedness, pauperization, and eviction from land often coincided with periods of scarcity resulting in a dramatic rise in the crime rate in the North-Western Provinces and Oudh between 1875 and 1886, as Table 3 shows. (The rate was, however, to increase even more from 1886 to the end of the century.) The Government of India noticed that increase in the crime rate and expressed an alarm. But the Government of India saw no correlation between the new socioeconomic changes, poverty, and crime. Rather, it was of the opinion that the marked increase in the "growth of lawless spirit among the people" was due to the "seriously and increasingly defective" administration of criminal law in the provinces.[36]

TABLE 3: General Increase in the Crime Rate of the Provinces between 1876 and 1886[37]

Year	Total Number of Population	Number of Prisoners at Beginning of the Year	Number of Prisoners Received during the Year	Total Number of Prisoners per Year
1872	42,626,990			
1876		29,406	51,610	81,076
1877*		27,783	63,772	91,555
1878*		32,257	88,223	120,480
1881	44,876,499			
1885		20,177	81,825	102,002
1886		19,353	86,616	105,969
1887		20,763	93,639	114,402
1888		21,271	95,529	116,800
1889		22,912	98,067	120,979
1890		24,647	102,926	127,573
1891**	47,682,197	26,864	110,743	137,607
1892**		28,623	93,325	121,948
1893		26,521	97,331	123,852
1894		26,809	98,982	125,791
1895		29,221	113,689	42,910
1896*		32,195	108,986	141,181
1897*		35,595	133,519	169,114
1901	48,746,793			
1906		22,437	32,357	54,794
1907*		22,203	31,144	53,347
1908*		22,429	38,208	60,637
1909		24,556	31,233	55,792
1910		23,937	29,775	53,712
1911	47,997,364			

* Years of famine
** Years of scarcities

Of the thirty-five or so officers consulted in the North-Western Provinces and Oudh on the question of increased crime rate, nearly all confirmed that "crime [had] either increased or [had] a tendency to do so," but most felt that part of the increase was due to "better reporting" of crime.[38] Other chief causes enumerated for the increased crimes were: the inefficiency of the police; the non-deterrent character of the jail administrators; the lenient nature of sentences passed, most especially of habituals; the increased employment of native magistrates and the decrease of European ones; and the inefficiency of the prosecuting agency in courts.[39]

The Commissioner of Sitapur Division reported that crimes that increased considerably were "ordinary theft" and "burglary, technically known as housebreaking or house trespass."[40] Why did those crimes increase? He cited a number of reasons: the rise in the price of food while the ordinary rates in labor wages remained unchanged; the increase in population; the increased means of communication giving criminals an easy escape from punishment; and the non-deterrent character of the punishment. He further explained, "the poor found it harder than it used to be to live by labour, and naturally a certain portion of them eke out the wages of labour by crime."[41] As for the non-deterrent nature of the punishment, he simply reiterated the position taken by the majority of the officers: "The Native Magistrates [were] far too apt to impose sentences inadequate for the offense, and fail[ed] too often to see the value of punishment as a deterrent of crime."[42]

The opinion of the Police Department did not differ. It noted that the native magistracy was indeed "neither so honest nor fearless as Europeans" and was prone to acquit criminal cases of all kinds. But the department was sure that the class of "Native Magistrates will improve." But more importantly, it noted:

> Government sometimes forgets that it has the means of repression, which do not involve the addition of permanent expensive establishments. The means of punishment may be more sternly used, and the form of punishment made more deterrent. . . . The humanitarian policy of the Government of India has for some time made imprisonment less and less of an effective punishment, but even such as it is, it might be more boldly used.[43]

An analysis of the report shows that aside from such contradictions as "better reporting" and "inefficiency of police," the crime rate was indeed on the rise. But while some recognized that "poverty" was the root cause of petty theft and house trespass, the most common crimes of poverty, the treatment prescribed, however, was very much in keeping with the colonial policy of "repression." Defects were found to exist in the law enforcement agencies and in the penal system which were to be corrected. And most of all, the "weakness" and the "corruption" of the native magistrates were emphasized in contrast to the "honesty" of the British officers who did not hesitate to inflict punishments upon the poor masses. The objective of the inquiry was, of course, to find and correct the weaknesses in the law enforcement and criminal justice systems to repress crime and to punish criminals. An improvement in the material condition of the masses, the root cause of crimes, was not a part of the inquiry even though the Commissioner of Sitapur had noted and, as the Inquiry of 1888 was to confirm later,[44] that the food prices had risen while ordinary wages had remained unchanged.

The Inquiry of 1888 was requested by the Government of India in response to two allegations. The first allegation came from Sir W. W. Hunter in 1887, who stated that "the remaining fifth or 40 millions of the population of India go through life on insufficient food."[45] The second assertion came from Sir Charles Elliot when he wrote, "I do not hesitate to say that half of our agricultural population never know from year's end to year's end what it is to have their hunger satisfied."[46]

The findings of the Inquiry of 1888 supported the allegations and made further relevant points. The Commissioner of Allahabad Division, for instance, wrote, "Commissions have sat, have elaborated voluminous reports, and in consequence the idea has become pretty general that the poorer classes of the agricultural population have not much to come and go on, that a short harvest or high prices means a reduction in a not too liberal food scale."[47] For Banda District he added, "I believe there is here very little between the poorer classes of the people and semi-starvation; but what is the remedy?"[48]

And to emphasize the degree of destitution, he cited the increase/decrease in population rate for the following districts: Allahabad, Jaunpur, Cawnpore, Fatehpur, Banda and Hamirpur (see Table 4).

What the figures revealed was that, in sixteen years, population increased substantially in Jaunpur only. (The explanation was that Jaunpur suffered less from famine.) Allahabad showed a decrease and then some increase; Fatehpur remained practically the same; and in Cawnpore, Banda, and Hamirpur, the population decreased and remained below the level of 1865.[49] The Commissioner linked this decrease of population to peasant destitution and hunger.

The Inquiry further showed that the condition of the lower classes of people in Oudh was particularly bad. One official reported that in Oudh " the custom of serfage [was] still general." They had borrowed money and had bound themselves to serve, " they and their heirs after them, till the debt [was] paid."[50] Another official from Eastern Oudh reported that if one were to " walk around any Oudh jail on a Sunday morning . . . you will see a very low average of stature, physique and health. This was undecidedly so for the want of more and better food."[51] His observation linked hunger to crime and imprisonment.

TABLE 4: Increase/Decrease in Population Growth of Various Districts between 1865 and 1881[52]

Year	Allahabad	Jaunpur	Cawnpore	Fatehpur	Banda	Hamirpur
1865	1,403,045	1,015,427	1,192,836	681,053	726,277	520,941
1872	1,394,245	1,025,869	1,155,439	663,815	697,611	529,137
1881	1,474,106	1,209,663	1,181,396	683,745	698,608	507,337
Population Growth +/- between 1865 and 1881	+ 71,061	+ 194,236	- 11,440	+ 2,692	- 47,669	- 13,604

Although this inquiry did not correlate poverty to crime either, it did illustrate the destitution and semi-starved condition of the masses and the prevalence of petty theft during this period. For instance, while the enormous number of 29,775 cases of theft reported in Oudh during 1868–1869 was an effect of famine,[53] the high number, as Table 5 of other years shows, resulted from low wages, high prices and scarcities.

TABLE 5: Reported Number of Grain Thefts in Oudh, 1869–1875[54]

Year	Number of Thefts
1869–1870	15,259
1870–1871	12,429
1872–1873	23,662
1873–1874	21,286
1874–1875	16,202

Tables 6 and 7, on the other hand, illustrate the consistent low wages and the rising cost of food prices in the period that contributed to the high crime rates, as noted by the Commissioner of Sitapur.

TABLE 6: Quinquennial Variations in the Wage Rates for Cawnpore, Fyzabad, and Meerut[55]

Years	Cawnpore	Fyzabad	Meerut	Average Wages for the Three Districts
1873	100	100	100	100
1873–1875	100	86	107	98
1876–1880	102	78	111	97
1881–1885	101	70	113	91
1886–1890	110	70	122	101
1891–1895	112	70	122	101
1896–1898	109	71	99	90

Notes: The rates for the second half of 1873 are being taken as = 100. It is important to note that these wages were for "able-bodied laborers" *only.*

The first table shows that the wages of "able bodied laborers" varied from one district to another. Nonetheless, during the twenty-five years, the average wages in the provinces remained below or around the 1873 level. But these were only for able-bodied laborers. No matter how the term "able-bodied" may have been defined, it is clear that women laborers would not have been included in this category. Their rate of wages, needless to say, would have been much lower.

The second table, on the other hand, shows that, with the exception of a few years in the early 1880s, food prices rose consistently. In fact, there was a dramatic rise in food prices from the mid-1880s to the end of the century. High food prices and low wages added to the distress of the masses, and severe punishment did not impede the increasing crime rate. The crime rate, however, did decline after the turn of the century. There is no evidence to show that there was a marked improvement in the material condition of the peasant classes after 1900. This decline in crime rate may be attributed to a combination of factors.

Population decline was one, an appreciable decline began before 1900, as Table 4 shows. Whether this change in population had any effect on decreasing the crime rate cannot be definitely established. Another possible explanation may, however, be that with the independence movement gaining momentum during this period, the attention of the rulers and the law enforcement agencies became focused on political insurgents rather than on women's crimes and on general thefts of a minor nature.

While economic changes and social formation were the major contributing factors to peasant poverty and crime, commercialization of agriculture did no less than to add to the distress of the peasant. The Indian modes of agriculture were seen by some officials as the "dregs of an old world barbarism," and the remedy was to modernize this "barbarity" through commercialization.[56] Still, as other writers show, Indian agriculture was to remain primarily "feudal throughout the colonial period."[57] This despite the fact that the Imperial Government, for its part, was also "committed from the outset to develop and distribute agricultural wealth on a scale hitherto unparalleled."[58] Such projects introduced by the government as canals and railways did indeed modernize and develop agriculture. But the problem with such innovations was that it did not help the peasant. Aside from causing ecological harm,[59] canals made the cultivation of crops highly selective.[60] For instance, from the 1870s, canals not only helped to introduce far more lucrative and "valuable" crops along the irrigated tracks,[61] but in many cases, canal irrigation replaced the cultivation of staple food grains on which the masses had depended for subsistence. Wheat, sugar cane, cotton, indigo, and opium, "all hitherto almost unknown in the area," replaced the older varieties of staple crops such as barley, jowar, puls-

TABLE 7: Variations in the Quinquennial Averages of Prices of Some Common Food Grains, 1861–1898[62]

	Years								
	1861–1865	1866–1870	1871–1875	1876–1880	1881–1885	1886–1890	1891–1895	1896	1897	1898

North-Western Provinces

Wheat	64	109	100	104	96	117	127	171	195	120
Rice	89	104	100	106	102	111	125	143	177	128
Barley	82	102	100	100	92	114	122	186	210	110
Jowar	84	97	100	99	84	115	115	163	193	108
Bajra	77	98	100	98	83	111	118	177	179	105
Gram	90	116	100	109	95	105	112	165	246	130
Arhar	66	79	100	104	89	78	87	132	200	124

Oudh

Wheat	77	106	100	107	9	120	137	184	205	127
Rice	87	114	100	113	102	115	125	145	186	130
Barley	72	97	100	98	92	116	133	191	226	108
Jowar	75	96	100	97	82	123	129	187	205	111
Bajra	81	96	100	100	83	117	125	195	199	112
Gram	79	108	100	106	97	103	114	164	247	124

Note: The prices of 1871–1875 are being taken as = 100.

es, and the like.[63] The same pattern of agriculture followed in Muttra, Shahjahanpur, Moradabad and in many other districts.[64]

And nor were the canals used for the irrigation of staple food crops that were being cultivated. In 1877, for example, even when the rains had completely failed, canal water was being used for the irrigation of more valuable crops of sugar cane, indigo, and cotton.[65] One official during the drought of 1877 noted that it was "a melancholy sight to see acre upon acre of magnificent indigo and sugar cane, while hardly a blade of any food grain was to be observed."[66]

Many districts, such as Muttra and Shahjahanpur, paid most heavily in the famines of 1868–1869 and 1877–1878,[67] not only for the cultivation of cash crops, but also for large exports of food grains to provinces that had already suffered harvest failures, and also to Europe depleting the store and converting a scarcity into the devastating famine of 1877–1878.[68] Moradabad and Ghazipur suffered the same fate in the famine in 1896–1897.[69] While the export of grains from the provinces may have been an insignificant percentage in the overall export, it was, nonetheless, sufficient to deplete the stock and to raise food prices adding more to the distress of the masses.

Economic severities and famines naturally caused loss of a phenomenal number of lives and a decline in the birth rate of the provinces as a whole.[70] It was the same landless class of field laborers, agricultural classes, and rural artisans who had constituted more than three-fourths of the population, that became victims of repeated starvation and death.[71]

In Muttra alone, for instance, the total number of deaths from July 1877 to December 1879 amounted to 112,825.[72] And from Shahjahanpur, the Secretary to the Famine Commission reported:

> But the chapter of the official report which deals with the mortality is the one which has the most melancholy interest, and, imperfect as the returns are, there can be little doubt that figures tell only too true a tale of deplorable suffering and death. From November 1877 to October 1878, 60,695 persons were returned as having died out of a total (by the Census of 1872) of 949,471. . . . I have myself seen villages in which hunger followed by fever, had killed off 75% of the population, Chamars, Kisans, etc., who lived by day labour.[73]

According to the Famine Commission's estimation, there was an excess of 1,250,000 deaths in the Province as a whole in 1879.[74] But the record of the famine years of 1896–1897 was worse when reportedly 1,505,737 perished.[75] The overall consequence of the repeated severe economic distress in the thirty-six districts of the provinces was that the death rate gradually exceeded the birth rate[76] between the years 1872 and 1921, as Table 8 shows. This means that in approximately forty years, between 1872 and 1911 (the period of this study), the population of the provinces apparently grew by 5,350,374 persons. Whether the growth of about five and one-half million persons in forty years can explain the theory that a "rapid increase" in the population rate caused pressure on land, unemployment, poverty and hunger which increased the crime rate[77] is a debatable point. The officials, however, continued to explain the lack of employment in terms of "overpopulation" during the last half of the nineteenth century. And, they felt that emigration "relieved" the provinces of only about 590,000 persons between 1887 and 1897.[78]

TABLE 8: Population of the North-Western Provinces and Oudh under Registration, 1872, 1881, 1891, 1901, 1911, and 1921[79]

Year	Total Population under Registration	Increase/Decrease
1872	42,646,990	
1881	44,876,499	+2,229,509
1891	47,682,197	+2,805,698
1901	48,476,793	+ 794,596
1911	47,997,364	- 479,429
1921	46,510,668	- 1,486,696

The emigration of male labor, too, was directly related to the economic changes, indebtedness and distress, and not to overpopulation, as was maintained by some officials. Though the exact extent of emigration was not known, it was estimated that the movement of population—both internally and beyond India—was very great. There was, thus, at all times an appreciable proportion of the male population absent from the provinces in search of employment far afield.[80]

Emigration beyond India to the developing colonies of the British Empire, which served dual purpose, was also considerable and, it appears the provinces provided the largest number.[81] Long-term emigration, on the one hand, eliminated the danger from below from unemployed "bad characters" and "criminal population," as one District Officer explained: "the campaign against the bad characters . . . has not been unfruitful of results. Increased vigilance and more efficient patrol on the part of the police has had the *usual result of causing an actual emigration from among the criminal population.*"[82] On the other hand, this type of cheap labor migration formed a "part of a system of imperialist-imposed exploitation"[83] in the capitalist accumulation process. And the purpose of recruiting male laborers as single men was to avoid paying men family wages to reduce costs. But if the migration of male members abroad raised profits for European industries in Europe, then the low wages paid to the wives who remained behind, enabled the moneylenders, landlords and merchants to accumulate profits at home.

The problem, however, even with the "temporary nature of Indian male labor migration" abroad, was the separation of families from five to ten years (at least in the case of their emigration to Fiji). Laborers were assured a return passage only after completing five years of indentured labor with an additional five years of residency in the colony.[84] But those who chose to begin a new life in the land of their adoption never returned home.[85]

The above, somewhat lengthy discussion of the socioeconomic transformation created by the colonial political economy has been necessary in order to establish how peasant poverty, their evictions from land, scarcities, famines, commercialization of agriculture, emigration of male labour, and women's crime were all interrelated. That also meant that as the economic means for daily survival decreased, the prison population increased. How that process affected women and their crime pattern, is discussed below.

Socioeconomic Changes, Women, and Crime

There is, on the whole, little information on the actual condition of the nineteenth-century lower castes and classes of working women who suffered the most in the continual and prolonged pattern of socioeconomic dislocation. They were only barely included in government inquiries; in fact, in 1882, when the Government of India requested inquiries into the condition of the tenants in Oudh, the Provincial Government had specifically directed its Deputy Commissioners to examine "agricultural day laborers, but (*males*) only."[86] Consequently, a large number of women—widows and deserted wives, female agricultural and other laboring classes, who were the sole supporters of their families—were deliberately omitted from the inquiry. The interpretation of their contribution as "subsidiary to the occupations of their men," or as supplementary to the income of men,[87] meant that they were not considered actual workers when in fact their unrecognized form of labor formed the basis of their subsistence economy.

This one following account of some low castes and classes of women illustrates the precarious nature of their living:

> We are mostly widows, Chamarins, Lodhins, and other low castes. We depend chiefly on what we can get by fuel-gathering. When we don't

gather fuel, we work for cultivators in our villages. We weed, hoe sugar-cane, or reap. There is generally work of some sort to be had, and as long as there is work, we can manage to live. We have one meal a day in the evening. We eat whatever grain happens to be the cheapest. We don't always get enough to eat, and sometimes we don't have a full meal in twenty-four hours. Prices are so high that it is hard to live.[88]

Their narration reveals the marginal and unsteady nature of their employment. While this could also be explained in terms of pre-existing gender and class specific conditions, poverty and chronic state of their hunger, however, was an effect of high prices of food and the low wages of the working classes during this period.

But generally, it is not known what happened to women who may have lost their families through evictions or in famine related deaths; or what effect the colonial all-male emigration policy had on women and families; and what happened to the thousands of wives whose husbands died in the colonies or chose not to return. How did they support their children and themselves, particularly when severe economic conditions prevailed in the provinces with famines and scarcities occurring every decade during the last half of the nineteenth century? (Severe scarcities occurred in 1874, 1880, 1891–1892 and 1899; famines in 1860–1861, 1868–1869, 1877–1878, 1896–1897, 1908–1909, and 1913–1914.)

It can be speculated that some were economically and sexually exploited in the work place, some became prostitutes, while others committed adultery and other serious crimes for survival. It is, therefore, not strange to find jail records showing increased number of female criminals during the last half of the nineteenth century. They were products of the socioeconomic changes; women who may have lost their families and homes and had no means of support.

In fact, one classic court case in 1908, a year of famine, thoroughly illustrates the far-reaching social and criminal consequences of the economic changes that were taking place. The case involved a deserted woman with children whose husband had emigrated. The twenty-five-year-old wife enticed a ten-year-old girl to a disused well. She took her cheap jewelry, worth a few rupees, pushed her into the well and killed her.[89] On September 16, 1908, when she petitioned the Government of India for mercy from her sentence of death, she denied the charge against her. She told the court that her husband had brought her from Colombo and after a year he returned to Colombo leaving her behind with children. Her parents were also in Colombo and she had no one in that place to bring as witnesses. After deliberating the case, the Government of India also noted that the "petitioner was penniless and too poor even to engage a pleader." Her husband had indeed deserted her and she had no one to help her. And after observing, "We need not hang women except in very aggravated cases of murder," the court commuted her death sentence to transportation for life.[90] While her own life ended in transportation to the penal colonies, it is not known what happened to her children. It may, however, be fairly safely concluded that they too became street people, later to be labeled as "born criminals."

This account aptly depicts how the changing socioeconomic conditions and emigration affected women and their crime pattern. The crime of child-murder for cheap jewelry was not uncommon. The police reports of the North-Western Provinces and Oudh often noted such crimes committed by poor women (and men, of course). In one similar case, *Queen Empress vs. Nibbia*, Nibbia was convicted on her voluntary confession of child-murder for the sake of the child's ornaments.[91] In upholding her sentence of transportation for life, the High Court noted, "Unfortunately children were *frequently* murdered for their ornaments and in such an offense the person who had committed it, should not be dealt with leniently."[92]

In another case in Jaunpur, a Mussammat Misri was charged with the same crime and was executed in 1909.[93] These are only a few cases that, because they were appealed, have been preserved in the annals of the High Court records. However, as the judges had observed, the murder of children by women for jewelry was frequent.

These were some of the specific factors that made women's experiences under colonialism very different from those of their male counterparts and why they resorted to such crimes. Male peasants and laborers could not only often secure employment as daily wage earners, but they also suffered less exploitation and indignities. Moreover, they could abandon their wives and children and move about freely in search of a means of subsistence both under normal and adverse conditions. Women, on the other hand, suffered from lack of employment as well as economic and sexual exploitation; further, they were often burdened with children. Their movements were hindered both by dependents and social restrictions.

That also meant that abandoned women and widows often faced starving children alone during the famine years. While jail records suggest that such women's immediate reaction to scarcities was petty theft, many women also resorted to begging and to prostitution.[94] Many others either sold or abandoned their children.[95] And finally, as a last resort to escape prolonged suffering from starvation, some distressed mothers resorted to willful murder of their children and/or to murder-suicide. However, while mothers were more often guilty of the crime of murder and murder-suicide because of starvation, cases where fathers murdered their families were also known.[96] In Meerut, a correspondent was grieved to find that parents were obliged to kill their own children to relieve them of suffering and starvation.[97]

In one case, a woman killed her two daughters and one son with a knife, and then cut her own throat. But she survived. She explained that she thought it was advisable to kill the children to save them from suffering before she took her own life.[98] In Hamirpur, on July 10, 1895, one Mussammat Makhania, unable to support herself, jumped down a well with her child in her arms. She was taken out alive but the child was dead. The woman was sentenced to ten years' rigorous imprisonment.[99] In Azamgarh, on October 12, 1895, a Mussammat Mahdai, through sheer deprivation, took her two daughters in her arms and jumped down a well. She and her elder daughter were rescued but the younger one drowned. The woman was given two years' rigorous imprisonment.[100] Mussammat Ajuba, on October 31, 1888, in Fatehgarh, "being in great want," threw her child into a well. It is not known what punishment she was awarded.[101] In Gorakhpur, on June 23, 1895, Mussammat Phatingia threw her child into a well on account of poverty and distress. She was sentenced to five years' rigorous imprisonment.[102]

The exact number of suicides is nowhere stated, and it would be impossible to compilate. When thousands were starving to death, who could decide how many committed murder/suicide and how many simply died of starvation? Nonetheless, 13,317 suicides between 1876 and 1886[103] will have to serve as the number to illustrate that there was a correlation between famine and murder/suicides and abetment of suicides. The highest number of suicides occurred during the famine years of 1877 and 1878, when many starving mothers "did away with their children whom they despaired of nourishing."[104] The police report of 1877 also noted the increased number of cases of exposure of infants (leaving infants unattended), attempted suicides, and with them, the increased number of convictions. The report linked the increase of those crimes to the destitution caused by great distress.[105] It thus firmly established those crimes, with theft and dakaiti, as offenses relating to severe economic deprivation.

And finally, it would seem that mother-murderesses perceived their situation as one of a prolonged starvation and an eventual painful death. To them, suicide was a way to relieve suffering. The state, on the other hand, merely interpreted their crimes in terms of law and order and punished those who survived their attempts at suicide. The justice system's focus on "law and order" often masked the real cause of women's crime: their destitution. Suicides and abetment of suicides, and the prosecution of mothers, again illustrate how the colonial experiences of women differed from those of men. The mothers were not only left alone with starving children, but ultimately, when they found it necessary to commit gruesome crimes, they were also left alone to face the law. Crime of murdering starving children, murder-suicide and abandonment of children were immediate consequences of famine years. And, although petty theft and prostitution appear to have been the most common long-term poverty related offenses of women (prostitution is discussed in Chapter 3), there were, however, other serious crimes committed by them. Poisoning, for example, was practiced by women to a great extent, as a police report noted in 1906: "The most glaring point in reading the reports of districts was the degree in which women were addicted to the crime of poisoning."[106] According to reports, vengeance and jealousy were the chief motives where women used poison as a murder weapon within the domestic circles. In such cases, family members and spouses were their victims.[107] But who were those other semi-professional and professional women poisoners? Where did they come from? And why did they go around poisoning people?

Again, no specific information is available. But from certain statements—such as "among 727,892 indefinite and nonproductive class of persons were 442,522 women" who formed "numerous hordes of beggars that infested Allahabad"[108]—it is not difficult to speculate where female poisoners, prostitutes, and kidnappers came from. Allahabad was a place of pilgrimage for travelers and beggars alike. More than likely, the situation in other places of pilgrimage, such as Benares, was no different. Those women, who infested such places were abandoned wives, widows, and victims of evictions from their lands. Although the Secretary to Government, North-Western Provinces, and Oudh, felt that such "ordinary beggars, houseless women, destitute laborers and impoverished cultivators are not by habit breakers of the law,"[109] he did not specify how these classes earned their living. It is obvious from his observation, however, that large classes of houseless women, destitute laborers, and impoverished cultivators existed in colonial India as shifting hordes of beggars. And those female criminals who made their living through roaming the length and breadth of the provinces poisoning innocent people and taking off with their belongings were from those "numerous hordes of beggars." For instance, during the year 1884, of the total prisoners admitted in jails in the North-Western Provinces and Oudh, 4,452 men and 203 women were recognized as old offenders and habituals.[110]

One such offender was Musammat Parbuti, a Rajputan, who had been released from Agra jail in 1874 after five years when she was rearrested in Benares for the same crime. She was transported for life.[111]

In 1877, when Miriam of Saharanpur (apparently a well-known poisoner) was captured, she related how she fed her victims sweet cakes laced with poison. When they became insensible, she made off with their money. She robbed one family while pretending to be a midwife.[112] In another case, in 1883, an old Brahmani accompanied by her son met four men in Mainpuri. One of the men was looking for a bride. The Brahmani promised to find one for him and accompanied them. On the way, she drugged them all and disappeared with all their money and belongings, leaving three corpses behind. Another woman in Lucknow poisoned her own brother-in-law and his wife with *puris* (fried bread) and then robbed them.[113] In Gonda, a woman was convicted of poisoning an infant for the sake of its ornaments.[114] In Bulandshahr, another woman was convicted for committing two offenses of poisoning for the sake of robbery.[115] Old women sometimes took young boys with them to train them in the art of poisoning. One Brahmin boy who was trained by a woman, for instance, had committed his fifth crime of poisoning by the age of twelve.[116]

These are only some cases of women poisoners, but the examples chosen here illustrate a number of points. There were "habitual" women poisoners who went about decoying, drugging, murdering, and robbing people; some of them did not hesitate to murder several people at any one time simply to get away with their belongings. [117]

The second form of female crime that strikes one in reading the criminal returns of the North-Western Provinces and Oudh is kidnapping. The incidence of kidnapping was not much lower than that of the crime of poisoning.[118] The case of Mussammat Subboo, a Chattrin of Allahabad and a kidnapper, shows how some professional women moved about kidnapping. She was convicted in 1850 in Oudh, in 1857 in Meerut, later in Punjab, and again in Oudh in 1874.[119] There were others like Mussammat Subboo, as the 1874 report shows. Of the total number of 192 kidnappers arrested, fifty-eight were women.[120]

Women kidnappers often worked in groups criss-crossing the provinces. But when they associated with men for kidnapping and abduction of girls,[121] their task was to make the acquaintance of the usually innocent and unsuspecting victims. They opened up ways for "enticing away victims by painting attractive pictures of a change in life." [122] No other information is available on the lives of women poisoners or kidnappers. But from what little there is in the jail reports, it is clear that women committed minor as well as major types of crimes. Nor was poisoning and kidnapping confined to any particular caste of women. Brahmin and Khatriya women, both belonging to the higher castes, moved about as freely and in as many numbers committing crimes as did the women of the lower castes.

The higher caste women criminals, however, are of particular interest. Because they generally practiced seclusion, and had the cultural ideology of "respectability" associated with them, it comes as a surprise that some would so freely move about and indiscriminately mix with different types of people committing crimes. One explanation might be that they, too, were victims of their changing socioeconomic circumstances.[123]

The plight of another group of females, the women of the "criminal" tribes, further demonstrates the fact that women's criminality was in part a product of the deliberate capitalist policies of the government, and in part of the impact of modernization and progress.

The "criminal tribes" as a people divorced from land had long histories. The case of three criminal tribes, the Banjaras, the Chain Mullahs, and the Pasis, show how all (who were otherwise not criminals)[124] were driven into committing crimes for survival as each lost its traditional means of support.[125] The Banjaras, for instance, were the inland transport workers of India. For generations they had carted goods all over the country on their mules and donkeys. They had done the same for the British army during the wars they fought in India. But when roads were built and railways were opened, the Banjaras lost their traditional employment.

The second tribe, the Chain Mullahs, were the river transport carriers. They had transported goods and merchandise up and down the great waterways of India in their barges. But when canals were constructed, the water levels over hundreds of miles downstream fell so drastically that they could not continue their occupation, except during the monsoons.[126]

And finally, the Pasis, who had numbered over a million and constituted the largest tribe in the United Provinces. Flower gatherers and tappers of trees (mohuwa tree), they made liquor for their livelihood. But when the colonial law made distilling a state monopoly, they, too, lost their means of support.[127]

After losing their traditional occupations, these and other groups like them (either because the wandering tribes could not settle down, or they had no place to settle down) turned to crimes for livelihood.[128] They generally wandered in groups of ten to twenty families "under the leadership of a strong patriarch whose cunning and enterprise" held the families together.[129] One of those cunning ways was the use of their women to furnish tribal gangs with useful information as well as to lure men of other castes and tribes as recruits.[130]

However, because of not only their nomadic nature and criminality, but often even the mere suspicions they aroused, many adult males were continually being arrested and imprisoned. When on one occasion, for example, approximately 4,000 Barwars were brought under the provisions of the Criminal Tribes Act in 1884, it was discovered that 60 percent of their adult males had already undergone imprisonment.[131] With such large numbers of their men thus incarcerated, the leadership of the vagrant gangs of

North India fell upon their female members.[132] Through the latter part of the nineteenth century and into the twentieth, we find reports of families being attacked and robbed of their cash and jewelry by criminal tribes headed by females. One such group of the Sansiah tribe was reported to have roamed around and committed dakaitis in 1890 led by one Mussammat Passamah.[133]

In 1906, sixteen Beriahs belonging to Mussammat Paro's gang committed two dakaitis in the Mainpuri district where they were arrested.[134] In the same year, six gangs under female leadership were traveling long distances committing crimes. These gangs were known to be under the leadership of Mussammats Gyano, Waziran, Budhnim, Bataso, Kaoria and Gobindi, female gang leaders who usually began their journeys alone from the adjoining states. But as they entered the British territory, other men and women joined them. Apparently, they traveled principally by railways, covering extensive areas and committing dakaitis and robberies on the way. The gangs of Mussammats Waziran and Gyano were said to be the largest, but the latter committed more serious crimes than the other gangs. Her gang members were convicted for brutally murdering a village *chaukidar* (village watchman).[135]

The names of the female ringleaders have been deliberately mentioned not only to show that female leadership was not found only in isolated cases, but also to establish the relationship between their economic hardship and their criminal activities. The one bold and reckless incident in 1910 perhaps best illustrates the economic plight of the tribes: *for a quantity of rice*, ringleaders Mussammats Mangia and Hulaso and their gang beat some villagers even as they were being escorted by chaukidars.[136]

Regretfully, I could find no further information on any of the female gang leaders. It is not known where they came from, what the specific circumstances were that compelled them to assume the leadership of their gangs, or what were the results of their eventual encounter with the law. However, an account of a "round-up," when 1,236 men, women and children were surrounded by the police and taken into custody, tells us that all the adult males were taken and imprisoned for life at Sultanpur Jail. And some women "were assisted to emigrate to one of the colonies, with a chance of gaining a respectable livelihood."[137]

The point that comes through from this brief study of the females of the criminal tribes, however, is that their experiences and the experiences of the peasant women were not much different. In the case of the "criminal" tribes, the incarceration of the male members, often for life, caused severe economic plight obliging the female members to assume the responsibility for the tribes' survival. Thus, the policies and the activities of the colonial state often uprooted masses and made them criminals. In dealing with the social consequences of its own policies, the state also defined crimes and punishments on its own terms, labeled groups, and punished the guilty.

Another interesting feature of the colonial government's policy was its readiness to "assist women" either to emigrate to the colonies or to transport them to the penal colonies "with a chance of gaining a respectable livelihood" and so to "begin a new life." But the fact was that both the "coolie lines" in most colonies and the penal settlements in Port Blair and the Nicobars were nothing more than brothels. Therefore, they provided neither respect nor the anticipated better life to the women who were sent to those places.[138]

The conditions of the times were perhaps best summed up by this one official when he lamented:

> The history of famines in an agricultural district like Muttra is of great value in an enquiry into the effects of British rule. We have imposed peace where formerly war raged; we dispense justice with least impartiality, which can be said of no previous rulers; we have brought the blessings of easy modes of transit within the reach of all, and by our railways, canals and metalled roads an impetus to commerce, unequalled in the past, has been given; but if the condition of the people themselves has not improved, if population has declined and the increased wealth of the few has been purchased at the cost of the great mass of the people who are the actual tillers of the soil, our satisfaction at the spread of western civilization may well be tampered with anxious reflection upon the causes of these untoward phenomena. The startling fact, brought to light by the recent census, of a decrease in the population between February, 1872 and February, 1881—just nine years—amounting to no less than 110,770 in a population (according to the census of 1872) of 782,460, or at the rate of more than 16 percent, pre-supposes some potent and more than usually baneful influences at work. Chief among these was famine.[139]

The problem precisely was the class struggle and oppression of the lower classes. But the question was not so much the famine but the general semi-starved existence of the masses, even in the absence of famines. Economic changes and social formation were ushered in to meet the needs of the colonial state in formation. And the modernization of Indian agriculture through capitalism and commercialization only helped to accumulate the increased wealth of a few at the cost of many. Changes did not benefit the small cultivators; rather, they only intensified the poverty and semi-starved existence of the masses during the last half of the nineteenth century. Canals and irrigation replaced their staple grains with modern crops, and the railways carried away the available food even as the people starved.

Emigration of male laborers to far away places, like crime, was created by poverty and a semi-starved existence. But emigration, too, whether long-term or short, brought particular sufferings to women who were left behind to maintain traditional ties with their villages.

But rather than improving the economic system that produced criminals in increasing numbers, the colonial government directed its efforts towards making criminal administration more efficient so that more and more criminals could be convicted each year. In 1862, for instance, the reported annual crime rate was 108,934, and convictions were obtained in only 57 percent of the cases. In 1878, however, because of high prices and actual food scarcities throughout the provinces, the reported crime rate was 220,852 and convictions were obtained in seventy-five percent of the cases. This success of the conviction rate was attributed, with some satisfaction, to the system becoming much "more efficient" since 1862.[140]

But the futility of the high rate of convictions was well expressed in the view of the official above, because unless and until the economic conditions improved, the crime rates would continue to rise.

The purpose of this chapter has been to illustrate how crime was linked to economic distress of a large majority of the population. The social and economic dislocation that came with colonialism subjected the lower classes, men, women, and children to enormous stress. But women in particular paid a terrible price in that dislocation. They lost their traditional forms of mutual obligation and support; commercialization denied them benefits; and migration of their husbands in search of employment away from homes left them alone to support children. Overworked, ill-paid, abused, and exploited, many women, victims of circumstances beyond their control, became criminals when they sought to solve their problems the only way they knew how.

NOTES

1. *Jail Administration Reports, Judicial (Criminal): North-Western Provinces and Oudh for the Year 1895*, no. 511A of 1896 (Allahabad: Government Press, 1896), p. 2. (Hereafter cited as *Jail Reports. Jail Reports, Judicial (Civil)* will be specified as such each time.)
2. *Jail Reports for 1897*, no. 3897-H-18 of 1898, p. 33.
3. Ibid.
4. *Jail Reports for Year 1877*, no. 71 of 1878, p. 2.
5. *District Gazetteers, United Provinces, Pilibhit*, vol. XVIII, ed. H. R. Nevill (Allahabad: Government Press, 1909), p. 113. (Hereafter cited as *District Gazetteers.*)

6. As Bill Rau has argued in the case of some newly independent African countries; famines are man-made, a result of political and economic dominance of a small group of people which began centuries ago in colonial period. Bill Rau, *From Feast to Famine: Official Cures and Grassroots Remedies to Africa's Food Crisis* (London: Zed Books Ltd., 1991), p. 1.
   In India, there were twenty-two famines under British rule between 1770 and 1900; that is within a period of 130 years. Romesh Chunder Dutt, *Famines and Land Assessments in India* (Delhi: B. R. Publishing Corporation, 1985; reprint, London: K. Paul Trench, Trubner), 1900.
   Famines had occurred in the eighteenth century when conditions were unfavorable because of wars and disintegration of the Mughal Empire. But the warring conditions had subsided by the second half of the nineteenth century after the British Imperial Government firmly established its power. And yet this period saw perhaps the greatest number of famines and periods of scarcities.
7. Figures have been compiled from *Jail Reports for the Years 1876–1884 and 1895–1909*. Appendix 1. Statement II—Judicial (Criminal) (for Convicts only) "Showing the Religion, Age, Previous Occupation of the Convicts Admitted During Each Year"; and *British India Statistical Abstract, Criminal Justice*. No. 31. Distribution and Number of Prisoners in North-Western Provinces and Oudh. 1885–1886 to 1894–1895. Thirtieth Number. (London: H. M. S. O. 1896), p. 48. (Hereafter cited as *British India Judicial Statistical Abstract.*)
8. *Jail Reports*; and *British India Judicial (Criminal) Statistical Abstract for 1910–11 and Preceding Years*. Part IV (Calcutta: Government Printing Press, 1912), pp. 23, 24.
9. Kapil Kumar, *Peasants in Revolt: Tenants, Landlords, Congress and the Raj in Oudh*, p. 14.
10. Kapil Kumar, *Peasants in Revolt*, p. 4.
11. Ibid., p. 14; and Ranajit Guha, *The Elementary Aspects of Peasant Insurgency in Colonial India* (Delhi: Oxford University Press, 1983), p. 6.
12. Ranajit Guha, *The Elementary Aspects of Peasant Insurgency*, p. 6; and Kapil Kumar, *Peasants in Revolt*, pp. 12, 70.
13. Ranajit Guha, pp. 7, 8 and 71; Kapil Kumar, pp. 12, 70.
14. Ranajit Guha, *The Elementary Aspects of Peasant Insurgency*, p.7.
15. Jagdish Raj, *Economic Conflict in North India. A Study of Landlord-Tenant Relations in Oudh, 1870–1890* (Bombay, New Delhi: Allied Publishers Private Limited, 1978), p. 231.
16. Kapil Kumar, *Peasants in Revolt*, pp. 12, 17.
17. Jagdish Raj, *Economic Conflict in North India*, p. 73; and Elizabeth Whitcombe, *Agrarian Conditions in Northern India. The United Provinces under British Rule, 1860–1900*, vol. 1 (Berkeley, Los Angeles, London: University of California Press, 1972), pp. 50, 52.
18. Ibid., p. 21.
19. Shahid Amin, "Small Peasant Commodity Production and Rural Indebtedness: The Culture of Sugar-Cane in Eastern U. P., c. 1880–1920," *Subaltern Studies 1*, ed., Ranajit Guha (Delhi: Oxford University Press, 1982), p. 87.
20. Elizabeth Whitcombe, *Agrarian Conditions in Northern India*, p. 161.
21. Ranajit Guha, *The Elementary Aspects of Peasant Insurgency*, pp. 7–8; Kapil Kumar, *Peasants in Revolt*, pp. 22, 23.
22. *Revenue (Revenue) Department Proceedings*, "Report of the Agrarian Disturbance in the Partabgarh District," 1920, File No. 753/1920, pp. 10–11; and Kapil

Kumar, pp. 22, 23. The Proceedings was conducted in 1920 because of peasant unrest in Partapgarh District. The investigation, headed by Mr. Mehta, is, therefore, also known as *Mehta Report.* (Hereafter cited as *Mehta Report.*)
23. *Mehta Report*, pp. 10, 12.
24. *Mehta Report*, p. 15; and Percival C. Scott O'Connor, *The Indian Countryside. A Calendar Diary* (London: Brown Langham and Co., 1907), p. 266.
25. *Mehta Report*, pp. 5, 11.
26. *Weekly Notes of the Cases Decided by the High Court of the North-Western Provinces. Criminal Appeal No. 695 of 1887, Queen Empress v. Pohp Singh and Another* (Allahabad: Printed and Published at the "Indian Press," 19 December 1888), p. 643.
27. Jagdish Raj, *Economic Conflict in Northern India*, p. 245.
28. Kapil Kumar, *Peasants in Revolt*, p. 27. The population of Oudh in 1881 was 11,387,832. *Census of India*, U. P., Vol XVI, Part II, 1921 (Allahabad, 1932), p. 6.
29. *United Provinces of Agra and Oudh Administration (Revenue) Department Reports of the Revenue and Rent Paying Classes, 1903–1910* Chapter VIII (Allahabad: Government Press, 1917), p. 39.
30. *Mehta Report*, pp. 10, 12.
31. Gail Omvedt, "Migration in Colonial India: The Articulation of Feudalism and Capitalism by the Colonial State," *The Journal of Peasant Studies*, vol. 7, no. 2 (January 1980): 185–211.
32. Jagdish Raj, *Economic Conflict in Northern India*, pp. 73, 74.
33. Ibid., p. 73.
34. *Mehta Report*, p. 2.
35. Ibid.
36. *Judicial (Criminal) Department Proceedings*, "Administration of the Police and Criminal Justice in the North-Western Provinces and Oudh," 1889, File No. 311B, p. 87.
37. *Jail Reports*, No. 71 of 1878, p. 2; and No. 74 of 1879, p 2; *British India Statistical Abstract for the years 1885–1886 to 1894–1895*, p. 48; 1888–1889 to 1897–1898, pp. 74–75; and 1906–1910, p. 23.
38. Ibid., p. 29.
39. Ibid.
40. Ibid.
41. Ibid., p. 87.
42. Ibid., p. 88.
43. *Judicial (Criminal) Department Proceedings*, 1889, File No. 311B, pp. 87, 32.
44. *Board of Revenue (Revenue Settlement, Land Records and Agriculture) Department Proceedings*, "The Inquiry into the Condition of the Lower Classes of the Population, Especially in the Agricultural Tracts in 1887," 27 April 1888, No. 186, p. 1. (Hereafter cited as "The Inquiry of 1887 into the Condition of the Lower Classes.")
45. Sir William W. Hunter, *England's Work in India* (Madras, 1890), p. 80.
46. Sir Charles Elliot, in an article in *The Christian College Magazine* (October 1887), p. 281, quoted in "The Inquiry of 1887 into the Conditions of the Lower Classes," p. 2.
47. "Inquiry of 1887 into the Condition of the Lower Classes," p. 586.
48. Ibid.
49. Ibid., p. 158.
50. Ibid., p. 157.
51. Ibid., p. 160.
52. Ibid., p. 155.

53. *Oudh Administration Report,* 1868–1869, p. 18.
54. *Oudh Administration Report.* Figures have been compiled from different years.
55. Government of India, Statistical Bureau. Prices and Wages in India. Compiled under the Supervision of the Director-General of Statistics. Sixteenth Issue. Part III (Calcutta: Government Printing Press, 1899), p. 315.
56. C. W. McMinn, *Famine Truths, Half Truths and Untruths,* p. 189. Quoted in Elizabeth Whitcombe, *Agrarian Conditions in Northern India,* pp. 88, 89.
57. Gail Omvedt, "Migration in Colonial India," p. 204.
58. Whitcombe, *Agrarian Conditions in Northern India,* p. 8.
59. Ibid.
60. Ibid., pp. 8, 11.
61. Ibid., p. 8; and F. H. Fisher, ed., *Statistical, Descriptive, and Historical Accounts of the North-Western Provinces of India, Moradabad.* Vol. IX, Part II (Allahabad: 1883), p. 48 (hereafter cited as *Statistical, Descriptive, and Historical Accounts*); and Whitcombe, *Agrarian Conditions in Northern India,* p. 72.
62. Ibid., Part I. *Retail Prices,* pp. 132, 162.
63. *Statistical, Descriptive, and Historical Accounts. Ghazipur,* Vol XIII, Part II (1884), p. 19; and Elizabeth Whitcombe, *Agrarian Conditions in Northern India,* p. 71.
64. F. H. Fisher, J. P. Hewett, and H. C. Conybeare, eds., *Statistical, Descriptive, and Historical Accounts,* Muttra, Vol. III, Part I (1884), p. 49.
65. Ibid., p. 5.
66. Board of Revenue (NWP and Oudh), "Revenue Proceedings." Report of W. R. Burkitt, Officiating Collector, Etawah, November 16, 1877. Index no. 65, no. 140 (February, 1879); quoted in Elizabeth Whitcombe, *Agrarian Conditions in Northern India,* p. 74.
67. *Statistical, Descriptive, and Historical Accounts. Shahjahanpur,* Vol IX, Part I (1883), p. 46.
68. *Statistical, Descriptive, and Historical Accounts. Moradabad,* (1884), p. 49; and *Ghazipur,* (1884), p. 19.
69. *The District Gazetteer of the United Provinces of Agra and Oudh.* Vol. XVIII (Allahabad: Government Press, 1909), p. 62.
70. *United Provinces of Agra and Oudh Administration: Reports of the Vital Statistics and Medical Services.* Chapter VI (Allahabad: Government Press, 1908–1909), p. 36; and *Statistical, Descriptive and Historical Accounts. Shahjahanpur,* pp. 54–86.
71. *Statistical, Descriptive, and Historical Accounts. Muttra,* pp. 49–54.
72. Ibid.
73. *Statistical, Descriptive, and Historical Accounts. Shahjahanpur,* pp. 54, 86.
74. *The Administration of the North-Western Provinces and Oudh. Resolution on Famine Relief During the Years 1896 and 1897,* Vol. II (Allahabad: 1897), pp. 125, 138.
75. *The Administration of the North-Western Provinces and Oudh. Vital Statistics and Medical Services,* Chapter VI (Allahabad: 1908–1909), p. 36.
76. Ibid.
77. *Police Administration, Judicial (Criminal) Department. Report of the NWP and Oudh, Vital Statistics and Medical Services for 1908-1909.* Chapter VI, File No. 311B, p. 87. This study has discounted both the emigrating and immigrating population on the basis that outgoing and incoming persons balanced the number.
78. William Crooke, *The North-Western Provinces of India: Their History, Ethnology, and Administration* (London: Methuen and Co., 1887), p. 288.
79. *British India Statistics, Area, Population, Emigration, Births, and Public Health for 1911–12 and Preceding Years.* Compiled in the Office of the Director-General of Commercial Intelligence, India, Sixth Issue, Part V (Calcutta: 1913), p. 4.

80. Ibid.
81. *Statement Exhibiting the Moral and Material Progress and Condition of India* (during the years 1894–1895.) Chapter IV (London), p. 166; *North-Western Provinces and Oudh Administration Report for the Year 1894–95*, p. 45; and the *United Provinces District Gazetteers.* Vol. XXIII (1909), p. 84.
82. *North-Western Provinces and Oudh Administration Report for the Year 1894–1895*, p. 178; emphasis added.
83. Gail Omvedt, "Migration in Colonial India," p. 206.
84. Priyam B. Singh, *Fiji's Indentured Laborers, 1864–1920*, unpublished master's thesis, Concordia University, 1975, chap. 4, p. 99.
85. William Crooke, *The North-Western Provinces of India*, p. 288.
86. *The Inquiry of 1887 into the Condition of the Lower Classes*, p. 7; emphasis, but not parentheses, added.
87. *Census of India*, 1911, Vol XV, Part 1, pp. 401–402.
88. *The Inquiry of 1887 into the Condition of the Lower Classes*, p. 550.
89. Government of India (Home) Department. *A Collection of Important Orders and Precedents Relating to the Procedure Adopted in Dealing with Petition for Mercy from Condemned Convicts.* Progress. No. 113. 1885 August 1909. Dealing with *Proceedings on Petition for Mercy from Rahimathammal Under Sentence of Death in the Madura Jail.* October 1908, p. 391.
90. Ibid.
91. *High Court of the North-Western Provinces. Weekly Notes of the Cases Decided. The Case of Queen Empress vs. Nibbia (Criminal)*, Vol. IV, June 25, 1888 (Allahabad: Pioneer Press, 1891), pp. 133–135. (Hereafter cited as *Weekly Notes.*)
92. Ibid., pp. 133–135; emphasis added.
93. *Allahabad Law Journal. Containing Cases Determined by the High Court of Allahabad. Mussamat Misri versus King-Emperor.* (Criminal) Vol. VI (Allahabad: Government Press, 1909), pp. 839–846.
94. *The Bundelkhand Punch* (Jhansi), July 15, in *Confidential Selections,* July 28, 1896, p. 39; and *The Anis-i-Hind* (Meerut), August 12, in *Confidential Selections,* August 18, 1896, p. 436.
95. Ibid. Complaints against Christian missionaries were also lodged during the famine years. *The Rahbar* (Moradabad), for instance, observed that while in former times wolves and bears carried off children from their homes, but "now a new class of human wolves have come into existence, missing children of natives being frequently traced to the `den' of Christian missionaries." *The Rahbar* (Moradabad), July 5, in *Confidential Selections* for United Provinces only, July 16, 1895, p. 265.

And while *The Advocate,* (Lucknow) did not find fault with the missionaries for proselytizing children with every famine, as they did in 1896–1897 when they took a large number, it did register its disapproval of the government's handing over orphans to the institutions professing a different faith other than that of the children. *The Advocate* (Lucknow),in *Confidential Selections* for United Provinces only, January 16, 1902, p. 122.
96. *The Nasim-i-Agra* (Agra), 23 November, in *Confidential Selections,* November 30, 1896, p. 686.
97. *Jail Reports for 1906*, no. 4770 H-48 of 1907, p. 2.
98. Ibid.
99. *Jail Reports for 1907*, no. 7366 H-48 of 1908, p. 2.
100. *The Bundelkhand Punch* (Jhansi), August 19, in *Confidential Selections,* August 25, 1896, p. 443.

44 ■ ECONOMIC DEPRIVATION AND CRIMINALITY

101. *The Prayag Samachar* (Allahabad), August 27, in *Confidential Selections*, September 1, 1896, p. 472.
102. *The Anis-i-Hind* (Meerut), March 2, in *Confidential Selections*, March 11, 1895, p. 125.
103. Eustace Kitts, *Serious Crime in an Indian Province, Being the Record of the Graver Crime Committed in the North-Western Provinces and Oudh during Eleven Years, 1876-1886* (Bombay: Education Society's Press, 1889), p. 1. Kitts was a member of the criminal justice in the North-Western Provinces and Oudh from 1876 to 1888.
104. Ibid.
105. *Police Reports for 1878*, no. 739A of 1878, p.2
106. *Police Reports for 1906*, no. 354/1/249-07, p. 6.
107. Cecil Walsh, "Proof or Probability," *Crime in India*, pp 172, 173; and *The ILR*, Vol. XXX1, 1909, pp. 290, 293.
108. *Police Reports for 1874*, no. 820A of 1875, p. 38.
109. *Government of the North-Western Provinces and Oudh. Judicial (Criminal). Orders from the Secretary to the Government, North-Western Provinces and Oudh, to the Judicial Commissioners, Oudh.* (June 22, 1878), no. 896 of 1878, p. 4. (Hereafter cited as *Orders of the Government.*)
110. *Orders of the Government. From the Secretary to the Government, North-Western Provinces and Oudh to the Inspector-General of Police, North-Western Provinces and Oudh.* (1906) No. 354/1-249-07, p. 6.
111. *Police Reports for 1874*, no. 820A of 1875, p. 38.
112. Ibid.; and Eustace Kitts, *Serious Crime in an Indian Province*, p. 8.
113. Ibid.
114. *Police Report for 1874*, no. 820A of 1875, p. 38.
115. *Police Report for 1906*, no 354/1-249-07.
116. Ibid.; and E. Kitts, *Serious Crimes in an Indian Province*, p. 8.
117. E. Kitts, *Serious Crimes in an Indian Province*, p. 8.
118. *Police Reports for 1874*, no. 820A, p. 38.
119. Ibid.
120. Ibid.
121. *Indian Law Reports*, Allahabad Series, compiled by D. E. Cranenburgh, *Cases Determined by the High Court at Allahabad and the Judicial Committee of the Privy Council on Appeal from that Court*, Vol. XVII, 1896 (Allahabad: Government Press, 1909), pp. 290–293. (Hereafter cited as *ILR*.)
122. Eustace Kitts, *Serious Crime in an Indian Province*, pp. 7, 9.
123. Jagdish Raj, *Economic Conflict in North India*, p. 232.
124. *The Indian Police Collection*. MSS. EUR. F161. India Office Library. These papers were compiled by Sir Percival Griffiths for his work, *To Guard My People: The History of the Indian Police* (London: 1971).
   Much of the information on criminal tribes has come from S. T. Hollins, Inspector-General of Police, The United Provinces, 1931–1935. He served the Indian Police for over forty years. (Hereafter cited as *Indian Police Collection.*)
125. *Indian Police Collection.*
126. Ibid.
127. Ibid.
128. Ibid.
129. Ibid.
130. B. S. Bhargava, *The Criminal Tribes: A Socioeconomic Study of the Principal Criminal Tribes and Castes in Northern India* (Lucknow: Universal Publishers Ltd.,

1949), p. 85. It is interesting to note that the Salvation Army was involved in the rehabilitation and settlement of the Criminal Tribes. *Police Department Resolution No. 1177/VIII-33.* 17 September 1913. The economic conditions of those tribes which the government did settle on lands were often worse than the ordinary peasants and agriculturists. The moneylenders often charged them higher rates of interest leaving them in deep debt. The years of scarcity and famine brought them even greater sufferings. Bhargava, *The Criminal Tribes*, p. 85.
131. William Crooke, *The North-Western Provinces of India*, p. 140.
132. William Crooke, *Things Indian: Being Discursive Notes on Various Subjects Connected with India* (London: John Murray, 1906), p. 525.
133. *The Proceedings of the Annual Report on Special Crime for 1890 in North-Western Provinces and Oudh,* July 1891, File no. 527A, p. 37.
134. *Police Reports for 1905,* no. 1595/1-313-1905 of 1906, p.1.
135. *Police Reports for 1906,* no 354/1-249-07 of 1907, p. 9.
136. *Police Reports for 1910,* no. 366-VI-154 of 1911, p. 11.
137. *Proceedings of the Police Department for 1890,* "Annual Report on Special Crime for 1889," File no. 219A, p. 117.
138. For life in the coolie lines in the Fiji Islands, see Priyam B. Singh, *Fiji's Indentured Laborers.*
139. *Statistical, Descriptive, and Historical Accounts. Muttra,* Vol. III, Part 1 (Allahabad, 1884), p. 2.
140. *North-Western Provinces. Criminal Statements for the Year 1878* (Allahabad), p. 2.

2

Partiarchy, Colonial Rulers, and Women Criminals

Chapter 1 explored how many women victims of changing political, economic, and class relations came to be criminals in nineteenth-century colonial India. The main topics analyzed in this chapter are women victims of domestic violence and Hindu religious ideology who were made criminals by the native patriarchy in coalition with the colonial rulers; it also deals with some colonial laws and, the society—men and women— who helped to oppress the weakest segments of females.

Crime among Indian women was reportedly rare[1] in the colonial period; therefore, it comes as a surprise to learn that between 1875 and 1912, that is, in thirty-seven years, 165 female criminals were executed in the British North-Western Provinces and Oudh alone.[2] In England, on the other hand, forty-nine females were executed between 1843 and 1890, or in forty-seven years.[3] This means that more women than three times were executed in the North-Western Provinces and Oudh than were in England in forty-seven years. The population of the two geographical areas was approximately the same.

The often-noted low ratio of female criminality in the provinces, on the one hand, and the large number of their executions, on the other, though startling, was not incongruous with the colonial policy of using severe punishments to control crime. Lord Macaulay's suggestion in 1835 that "it [was] of the greatest importance to establish such regulations as shall make imprisonment a terror to wrong-doers" (because "death [was] rarely inflicted" in the country)[4] had failed as a policy and the jail population continued to show a marked increase. Therefore, Lord Ellenborough, in 1843, suggested that the death penalty and corporal punishment be used in more serious offenses to make criminals "examples for the society by punishing them severely."[5] This shift in attitude may explain the high number of female executions as the statistics from the Jail Reports show in Table 9.

The large number of executions in the years 1878, 1892, 1896, 1899, and

1909, as explained in Chapter 1, may have been due to murder and murder-suicide attempts during famines and scarcities of those years, although capital punishment does not appear to have been the rule in many of those cases. But economic hardships do not fully explain such executions as eight each in 1876, 1894, and 1895, six in 1900, or eleven in 1905.

Apart from those who were executed, there were others who were transported to the Andaman and the Nicobar Islands for heinous crimes as Table 9 and the following two reports from the Andaman and Nicobar penal colonies show.

Port Blair, 1861–1862:

Out of ninety-six female life-convicts who were permitted to marry ninety-six male life-convicts, fifty were transported for murder; sixteen either for accessory, accomplice or for abetting in murder; twelve for wilful murder; six for attempt to murder; five for robbery with murder; two for dakaiti; and one each for robbery, felony and infanticide.[6]

The Abstract of Crimes, Port Blair and the Nicobars, 1897:

Out of 709 women transported to the Andamans from all India that year, 609 were for murder, five for causing grievous hurt, five for poisoning, two each for abduction of females and child stealing, receiving stolen property, and house-breaking.[7]

Information on any of those women who received capital punishment or on those who were deported to the penal colonies was not available. However, according to jail reports, two groups of women—married women who jumped down wells to commit suicide and murdered their child/children in their arms in the process, and widows who murdered their illegitimate infants—formed the largest number of murderesses. This chapter deals with these two groups of women and their crimes.

These two forms of crimes have been chosen to explore partly because evidence, incomplete as it is, is available. Furthermore, these crimes illuminate quite well the relationship between the colonial state, native patriarchy, and women, on the one hand; and patriarchy, society, family structure, values, and women on the other. They also demonstrate how women's reactions to their abuse and violence turned them into criminals from victims.

Domestic Violence and Female Crime

Domestic violence is not new to history[8] nor is it specific to India. Nonetheless, women of India have formed an interesting theme of inquiry for almost two centuries. Most inquiries have centered on their gloomy conditions and their gross victimization in one form or another. One such

TABLE 9: Total Number of Female Jail Population, Number Transported to the Penal Colonies, and the Number Executed, 1875–1912[9]

	\multicolumn{7}{c}{Year}
	1875	1876	1877	1878	1882	1883	1884
Convicts	3,241	3,131	5,516	10,366	1,386	2,693	2,303
Transported		8	1	176	93	85	93
Executed	3			13	1	6	3

	\multicolumn{7}{c}{Year}
	1885	1886	1887	1888	1889	1890	1891
Convicts	2,151	2,499	2,592	2,636	3,106	3,126	3,773
Transported	103	103	87	94	95	98	116
Executed	1	1	0	6	2	2	4

	\multicolumn{7}{c}{Year}
	1892	1893	1894	1895	1896	1897	1898
Convicts	3,026	2,588	-	-	7,233	9,639	2,793
Transported	98	66	8	8	-	-	50
Executed	8	2	8	8	12	0	5

	\multicolumn{7}{c}{Year}
	1899	1900	1901	1902	1903	1904	1905
Convicts			854	1,905	1,830	1,568	1,714
Transported			50	34	6	43	24
Executed	5	6	6	4	4	6	11

	\multicolumn{6}{c}{Year}
	1907	1908	1909	1910	1911	1912
Convicts	1,576	1,761	1,356	1,429	1,252	1,100
Transported	36	34	33	25	34	28
Executed	3	3	5	4	3	1

contemporary thought has at least explained oppression against women in North India in terms of its "culture against females."[10] While it appears that violence against women was generally not a consistent practice across caste or regional lines in the nineteenth century North-Western Provinces and Oudh,[11] it is true that Hindu patriarchal culture has subjugated women.

An analysis of the traditional Hindu family structure reveals that various traditional patriarchal ideologies were devised to dominate women and to exercise control over them. Husband worship, submission, and subservience in a wife, it appears, comprised the accepted norm.

Notions of their inferiority and need to be dominated by men were impressed upon women as was the belief that it was against their true dignity to seek freedom. They were told they were most virtuous only when they surrendered all their rights and made no claims.[12] These teachings kept women subjugated economically, physically, and psychologically, and relegated them to an actual inferior status, lacking in respect and regard.

The result of teaching girls from their very childhood that as wives it would be their duty to perform every kind of service to benefit their husbands, their gods on earth, was that most Hindu girls grew up literally believing in that indoctrination and they served their husbands with an uncommon "scale of servile fear and capacity for endurance and toil."[13]

The code that applied to a Hindu husband in his relationship with his wife, however, was precisely the opposite. Patriarchy did not require that he greatly love or respect his wife,[14] with the result that there were homes where wives and women generally, in a domination/subjugation relationship, were treated poorly and punished for the slightest provocation or disobedience.[15] The society, too, both men and women, played its part in enforcing patriarchal and cultural norms in such ways as by acknowledging and supporting a husband's supreme authority over his wife no matter how cruel or how unreasonable, by keeping silent and withholding evidence even if he murdered his wife, and by upholding a woman's moral code and demanding her total purity while accepting a "man's sexual laxity."[16]

These above conditions applied chiefly to the high caste/middle class women who had economic security and lived a secluded life. The lower castes, agricultural and laboring classes who formed the large majority of the population, neither practiced high caste religious rituals nor lived in a joint family system. They were, however, not entirely free of patriarchal structure or domination/subjugation roles of gender relations in their homes and in society.

Strange as it might seem, women were not oppressed by men alone.[17] In extended families, it was not uncommon for older women to abuse the younger ones. Notwithstanding the fact that as a rule women suffered disabilities of all sorts—mostly uneducated and secluded in homes (high caste/middle class), and absolutely subordinated to men—still when they reached a certain stage in life, Hindu women became "avowedly powerful."[18] Then, as the mistress of the family, they "gained full power, controlled every event, great and small, and became an uncontrolled despot within the domestic circle."[19]

But sadly, these same old women as mothers-in-law generally exercised their full despotic powers over their young daughters-in-law and, in some homes, they became instigators of their murders and suicides. Such extraordinary accounts where a mother-in-law drugged her own daughter-in-law to bring about her prostitution so as to defame her and disown her,[20] or where another murdered her daughter-in-law because the "young woman was of dirty habits"[21] were not rare. In another case, a superstitious mother-in-law drove away her own newly married daughter-in-law into prostitution. She had feared the daughter-in-law might bring a bad omen to the family. By the time that young woman was eighteen, she was old and diseased.[22]

Though this power of the older women applied to the higher castes/classes in the extended family structure, the influence wielded by women of the peasantry and the lower classes who lived in nuclear families, was equally if not more marked.[23] When they gained an upper hand, they became unrivaled in their "scolding propensities [and] could pour forth volleys of abuse" on their husbands for hours and make the "whole neighbourhood ring with their loud, virulent and obscene railings."[24]

These practices were, in general, the accepted custom of the society with various degrees of domination/oppression of women. Nonetheless, in contrast to the views held by Anglicist/Missionary writers that all nineteenth-century Hindu women were generally unhappy and downtrodden, there was, in fact, another group of writers who gave quite the opposite picture. Other than describing the lower castes/classes of women as independent,[25] they found many high castes/classes of women "without doubt, happy, or at least contented, for they [were] taught at an early age that their condition in that regard [was] consistent with morals and religion. Many were excellent and devoted wives and mothers . . . and anxious parents who exercised their influence to keep order in their numerous households, which often comprised from fifty to a hundred more or less closely-related relatives."[26] The influence of women in property transactions, family affairs, "whether secular or religious, [was] very great."[27]

These writers also felt that "much sentimentalism [had] been needlessly expended on the Indian women. Like most women in other lands, she [was] not slow to give expression to the pathos of her life; but she, not less than her husband, would resent the belief that she is downtrodden and degraded,"[28] and, if anything, she was proud to follow her old ways.[29]

The dual position of Hindu women—their general oppressed position, on the one hand, and their place in society that did not differ much from women in other societies of the time, on the other—may be explained by noting that the overwhelming criticism of Hindu women's oppressed position generated by some Western writers overshadowed the fact that not all Hindu women were downtrodden. Nonetheless, while many women were quite content and happy in their lives, there were those who suffered extraordinary forms of violence even for ordinary everyday mishaps as police and jail records of the second half of the nineteenth century of the North-Western Provinces and Oudh show. "If the cakes were unbaked, the pulse burnt, the milk soured or the flour spilled, she [the young wife] was, not infrequently, made to suffer for the neglect in such extreme forms as branding and actual mutilation."[30] In one such case, when a man "reproved" his wife for wasting the household flour, she attempted to drown herself. But she lived to have her husband decapitate her because she had "brought shame on his family by attempting to drown herself."[31]

In other homes, murders of wives were committed when dinner was not prepared in time. In one case a thirty-five-year-old husband smashed the head of his fourteen-year-old wife with a heavy piece of wood;[32] in another case in Bareilly, a blind husband, when his dinner was not served on time, called his wife to his side, knocked her down, and beat her about her head with a thick stick until she died.[33]

Other wives suffered at the hands of jealous husbands who demanded their absolute subjection and implicit obedience as was illustrated in a village crime when a peasant woman with "fatalistic resignation" permitted her jealous husband to chop her head off with a mattock.[34] In yet another case, a villager slowly burned his wife to death with cowdung steeped in oil and plastered around her body.[35] The woman had been unable to account for an expenditure of five rupees which the husband jealously suspected she had given away to her brother. The woman had screamed in agony for thirty hours and, although four adult members of his family were present in the house all that time, not one made any attempt to save the woman's life.[36] In Ballia, a man decapitated his own mother who had received him somewhat coldly because of his misconduct with his younger brother's wife.[37] In another instance, in Fatehpur, a murdered woman's body was thrown into a well with her live infant. And although the villagers heard of the incident in the evening, they took no steps to rescue the unfortunate child till the following morning.[38]

The above examples illustrate some glaring forms of crimes against wives; wive's total subjugation; and the society's role in condoning husbands' complete domination, cruelties and murders of their wives. Since there are no records and statistics of the pre-colonial period, it is impossible to compare oppressions against women of the two periods. However, in a Hindu society where women (and everyone else) had their proper places, some violence to control disobeying and erring wives and women must have been exercised. But it would appear that as the impact of colonialism in the nineteenth century altered the family values, it also exaggerated some forms of violence against women.

While such reforms as the abolition of Sati in 1829, Widow Remarriage Act of 1856, and the general Western cultural influence led the orthodox patriarchy to strengthen its control over women, some colonial legislations did as much to encourage and to reaffirm patriarchal control, domination and oppression of women. For example, the clause "grave and sudden provocation" recognized it as unjust to punish men for their actions when they were themselves the victims of an irresistible impulse caused by "grave and sudden provocation."[39] When applied to adultery, the clause meant that if a man found his wife in the act of committing adultery and killed her, he would be acting while deprived of the power of self-control by grave and sudden provocation. His crime would then be manslaughter, not murder.[40]

What in fact this clause did was to reconfirm a husband's right to punish his wife, even murder, while at the same time it excluded man's moral deviancy from the law. It is not surprising, then, that the records show that accusations for "adultery," in particular against the lower castes/classes of women, had become fairly common in the courts. Nor would it be too farfetched to conclude that such laws must have led to the fabrication of adultery cases by husbands merely to punish wives.[41]

Another English law that was new to India, a legislation to uphold the conjugal rights of husbands, forced a wife reluctant to live with her husband with the threat of imprisonment.[42] This law, again, chiefly affected the lower caste woman who was neither as yielding nor as humble as a high caste woman. She earned independently and, if she decided to leave her husband and return to her father's house, she could do so.[43] But the new law not only deprived her of her freedom, it once again committed the gross injustice of not forcing a man to live with his wife against his will, in other words, this law, like the grave and sudden provocation clause, did not apply to husbands.[44] Thus, for women, the "English law had carried oppression still further, for it had imported a process from its own system previously unknown in India.[45]

How such laws might have encouraged serious crimes against women can be understood from the following two accounts. In 1890, in Shahjahanpur, an accused man confessed to following his wife and *repeatedly striking her with a lathi (a staff) until she died. He killed her because she persistently left his house for her parents' home*. He then dragged her and left her in a ditch of water. He was, however, acquitted by the Sessions Judge.[46] In the same year, in the same district, another man brutally murdered a woman with lathi blows because *the woman had refused to keep company with him* .[47]

It was against this background of domestic violence that *The Pioneer*, in a long article, "Suicides in India," brought the high statistics of suicide in the country to the attention of the government.[48] *The Pioneer* listed such motives for the crime of suicide as desperation and pressure from poverty, pain, grief, shame from violation of some village morality, and prolonged illness and the like.[49] But it also noted that they were young wives, the victims of family ill-treatment, who took a prominent place in the total number of suicides.[50] And the most common method employed by women was by drowning in the nearest village tank or well.[51] *The Pioneer* commented further that "if collected, the statistics of this favourite form of Indian suicide, especially by young wives, would be startling enough. But it was needless to say that they would not fully represent the facts."[52] And indeed, in addition to the very young wives' increasing number of suicide attempts by drowning, women with children were also jumping down wells, as was noted by the Inspector-General of the Police, North-Western Provinces and Oudh, in the Report of 1877.[53] Table 10 shows his findings of the large numbers of women who attempted suicide.

TABLE 10: Cases Reported of Attempted Suicide, 1871–1875[54]

	\ Year				
	1871	1872	1873	1874	1875
Males	288	188	257	231	163
Females	325	399	458	408	491

However, the colonial government's policies regarding women in domestic life was similar to its policies affecting them in economic life—one of disregard. That policy was evident in the reaction of the Chief Secretary to the Government when he directed the Inspector-General to give "some explanation on that crime." But he added, "It was, however, unnecessary in future to notice these subjects separately in your annual report."[55] With the Chief Secretary's directive, a decline in the suicide rate was reported with some satisfaction and with an observation that there indeed had been an "undue tendency to report instances of women falling into wells."[56] The justification given for the crime was that, in the heat of quarrel, women jumped feet first into wells where water was too shallow for them to drown, and where they had not intended to commit suicide in the first place.

However, in spite of the repeated encouragement given by the Commissioner to the Deputy Commissioners in Oudh to see that "more care will be taken in making such reports in future,"[57] the reported high incidence of

PATRIARCHY, COLONIAL RULERS, AND CRIMINALS   ■   55

women who perished by jumping down into wells with children in their arms did not diminish. Of the *reported* cases in 1885, forty-eight women perished with their infants while fifty-nine were rescued and were awaiting their trials. In 1890, seventy-six perished and eight were awaiting trials. In 1895, it was reported that the conviction of women for the murder of their children had increased from twenty in 1894 to twenty-nine in 1895. But the list by no means exhausted the cases of child murder by mothers, as ninety-two mothers had committed suicide at the same time by jumping down wells with their children. The Police Report of 1896 made a similar observation: "The number of cases of child murder does not seem to diminish much. In no less than eighty-one cases mothers committed suicide at the same time as murder by jumping down wells with their children."[58]

What made that offense twice as regrettable, as the police reports noted, was not only the dreadful frequency with which the crime was committed, but the loss of children's lives that occurred with it. They invariably died even when the mothers were rescued. Consequently, in cases where a child/children had died as a result of a mother's action, it was the crime of child-murder that took precedence over suicide, and, in that process, the woman's own reasons for seeking the ultimate violence against herself—suicide—was often lost, as the case of *Government vs. Musammat Chouree* in May of 1866 shows. In that case, the judges ruled, "Admitting that she committed the act whilst deprived of the power of self-control by grave provocation, still the provocation was not given by the child whose death was caused, nor was the child's death caused either by 'mistake' or 'accident.'"[59] Mussamat Chouree was herself sentenced according to the law, which required either transportation for life or capital punishment. (There is no record which it was in her case.) However, subsequent punishments for that crime, according to jail records, were often mitigated.

Suicide appears to have been a characteristic of the Indian society from early times,[60] but no punishment seems to have been prescribed for the "crime." Chances were that, under Hindu law, women who attempted suicide were rescued and their cases were either neglected and forgotten, or the Panchayats dealt with such cases within the village. Under the British Indian Penal Code, however, suicide (Section 309) was legally defined a crime and offenders were punished accordingly.

Labeling suicide victims of domestic violence "criminals," particularly when their violence was directed toward themselves (even with a child in arms), and punishing them, should have raised important questions. Whether they were true criminals or mere victims of their situations who sought a way out of their troubled lives was not determined; or who or what led them into committing suicide was not asked. And as it always followed, the instigators of the crime from whom women often sought their freedom escaped even interrogation, let alone punishment. And the police and the courts continued to record the victims of such murder-suicide cases as "guilty."

It is interesting to study the equivocal nature of the language in the Annual Criminal Statements showing the reasons why married women jumped down wells and how they were judged criminals. The entries invariably read: Woman jumped down a well in a "fit of anger." Woman jumped down a well in a "rage" with her child/children in her arms on account of a quarrel with her husband. A woman jumped down a well on account of a quarrel with her mother-in-law or her father-in-law, or simply on account of a family quarrel.[61]

Only very rarely do the records mention any specific factors such as a "husband's refusal to support" her or a husband's having "beaten" her, or that having been "grossly ill-treated" she jumped into a well with her infant.[62] In most cases, the very vague nature of the entries fails to inform who fought with whom, and whether or not women were abused before they decided to take their own lives. If anything, the reports leave the impression that the suicide victims themselves were always guilty of both quarreling and jumping down wells.

No doubt, there may have been some hysterical women who took the extreme step on trivial grounds. But it does seem strange that so many should have suffered from the same malady of "rage" and "fits of anger" under their peculiar circumstances and should have sought to commit suicide. The stereotyped nature of entries incriminating women for committing murder-suicide in a "fit of anger" might be seen as a similar biased condemnation of women as that implied in the statement that "women could not be raped unless they wanted to be raped."[63]

A more likely explanation in these suicide cases might be that women themselves were rarely asked to give an account of their criminal behavior. They were half dead when rescued, and were fearful, ashamed, and aggrieved at the death of their child/children. Furthermore, they were unable to defend themselves either from their own families, who were the cause of their suicide attempts in the first instance, or from the law. Thus, they too abided by the explanation handed out to the police. Moreover, the *chaukidar* and the police, who were also the products of the same social system, would find women guilty in any case. The result of turning the facts upside down was that women were made solely responsible for both the cause and the effect of their actions, and they were thus left to face the law alone.

But no written accounts are available to explain why mothers wanted to drown their children with them when jumping down wells to commit suicide. It can, however, be speculated that they may have been fearful for their children's welfare after their own death. It also appears that mothers attempted suicides more often with girls in their arms arousing the suspicion that unwanted girls by the family may have been yet another factor in the mothers' desperate crime. And finally, killing children, particularly a male child, may have been a form of retaliation against husbands for ill-treating them.

Whether or not the crime of murder-suicide by mothers was premeditated is not known. But, even though their crime was grave, they were not hardened criminals. They were trapped in their particular positions in life and, laboring against overwhelming mental, emotional, and physical pressures, they may have acted without thinking of the seriousness of what they were doing. Their suicide attempt was only a symptom of oppression and domestic violence.

The question of punishing those who attempted suicide with imprisonment was raised by the Inspector-General of Prisons of the North-Western Provinces and Oudh. He lamented the convictions of 427 persons in 1902 under Section 309 of the Penal Code (attempt to commit suicide).[64] Because such acts were usually committed under circumstances when the victims could hardly be aware of their actions, he contended, they should not therefore be held responsible for them. A much more humane proceeding, he felt, was to remove such persons to a hospital where they would have the benefit of treatment, as was being done in England.[65] He hoped, "Presumably, therefore, the principle of punishing such acts by imprisonment is not recognized at home, and I trust that practice will be more freely extended to India."[66]

But such "humane" practices were not common in India. Hospital treatment for one woman who suffered from fits of insanity would have been merciful. She had thrown three of her children into a well and was about to jump in herself when she was prevented from doing so. Instead, she was transported for life to the Penal Colony of Port Blair and the Nicobars.[67]

Widows as Criminals

Whereas the individual suicide offender—who was the sole victim of her own act, and who presented neither any threat to society nor to property—could be punished and easily forgotten; the widow could not. In India, the case of enforced widowhood had become entangled in religion and politics and widows became their victims.

This section, focusing on crimes committed by widows, shows how the issue of enforced widowhood, dominated by patriarchy and justified by religious ideology, became a problem of major proportions; why the colonial state was unable to abolish widowhood by legislation enforced by punitive measures, as it had done in the case of Sati in 1829; and how, because of a prolonged controversy, enforced widowhood actually became a colonial construct. And, so long as the orthodox patriarchy together with colonial rulers could persecute widows for all the social ills and incarcerate them in prisons, they could preserve their own sense of respectability and morality.

The problem of enforced widowhood was closely related to both Sati and child-marriages and they were all well established traditions when the British arrived in India. These customs, with the exception of child-marriages, were practiced mainly, though not exclusively, by some high castes/classes of Hindus such as Brahmans and Kshatriyas and then only in some parts of the country.

Widow, however, became the central figure who generated controversies right through the nineteenth century. Whether it was the issue of Sati—should a widow be burned on her husband's pyre; the issue of child-marriage—how child-marriages increased the number of widows; or the issue of enforced widowhood—whether or not it was to be abolished, all of them concerned the widow. The latter two controversies were to continue right through to India's independence.[68]

The life of high caste Hindu widows was, indeed, often deplorable as was observed by Pandita Ramabai, a Brahman widow and one of the earliest women reformers, "the poor, helpless high caste widow with the one chance of ending her miseries in the suttee rite taken away from her, remains as in ages past with none to help her."[69] The problem was that Hindu ideologies that explained widowhood was a punishment for sins of disobedience and disloyalty to their husbands in a previous life on earth, caused the society to often shun widows as sinners. Their psychological indoctrination and physical hardships of rigorous penance of strict diet, service to God, an austere life of piety, fasting, and devotion were all prescribed to atone for their sins. And to ensure chastity, it was impressed upon them that an unfaithful wife to her dead husband would be blamed here on earth and, would also be deprived of her place by her husband's side in the next world. But it is interesting to note that none of these ideologies applied to Hindu widowers. They remarried young girls no sooner than they buried their wives.[70]

In addition to their melancholy lives, many widows suffered varying degrees of abuses. The reasons for the contempt, especially of their female relatives, is not far to seek. The mother-in-law scorned the young widow who became the cause of her son's death—a son who was a source of her own social status and security. Moreover, in some joint-family homes, it was not uncommon for male members to pursue young unattached widows,[71] a practice which must have created friction and given women of the household another reason to scorn widows. It is, therefore, not surprisingly that it was the child-widow and young widow without children upon whom the wrath of the society fell most heavily. A widowed mother with sons, on the other hand, was often respected and the least shunned by society.[72] Though a sinner, she had at least fulfilled the most avowed object of her womanhood by becoming a mother of sons. A woman with daughters, however, did not fare as well.[73]

Another factor that made the condition of widows difficult was their economic dependence on others. According to Hindu law in North India, a widow could not inherit her husband's property; she only had the right of maintenance.[74] But the amount of maintenance was not regulated by any rules of law. And because in a joint-family a widow lived with her deceased husband's relatives, her maintenance depended mostly upon their pleasure.[75] Sometimes, however, it became the obligation of her sons to support her, but, in either case, a widow found herself in a helpless state and at the mercy of others for economic survival.[76] This law applied generally to most parts of the country, except to Bengal where a different school of Hindu law entitled a widow to inherit her husband's property.[77]

But what brought the reformers to focus their attention on enforced widowhood after Sati was abolished was not so much the widows' hardship or economic dependence on others. Rather, it was the issue of illicit sexuality and crimes that became associated with widows that alarmed them. The problem was that as the widow population grew, so did the "immoral" practices. In 1819, for instance, the calculated number of widows in India was 1,000,000 of the total population of 100,000,000, which meant that there was only one widow in every 100 of the total population[78] (or approximately one in forty to forty-five of the total female population). According to the Census of 1881, however, widows numbered at a staggering figure of 20,938,626 of the total population of 228,867,402, making every fifth woman in India a widow.[79] The widowers, on the other hand, numbered 5,691,937, which meant that only one man in every twenty of the male population was a widower. By 1901, the actual number of widows had increased to 25,891,936.[80] Their number grew, however, not because millions of widows might have committed Sati if Sati were not abolished, but because of several interrelated factors.

It would seem that the higher castes and classes of orthodox patriarchy, who had neither reconciled themselves to the suppression of Sati nor to the interference by aliens in their religious matters, strongly restated their position by making widow-marriage a sacrilege.

Another factor was the reconstitution of the custom of enforced widowhood under the colonial rule.[81] That is, the prolonged debate in the country right through the second half of the century brought on by the failure of the government to deal effectively with the issue of enforced widowhood, taught the custom to many lower castes and classes who did not practice it before, to practice the custom to enhance their status,[82] thereby increasing the number of widows. In the North-Western Provinces and Oudh, for instance, the Brahmans, the Khayasthas and the other high castes had the highest proportion of widows around 1910. Ten years later, the Pasis, Bhangis, Charmars, and Dhobis all had appreciably more widows.[83] Enforced widowhood, like Sati before it, had become a status symbol.

The third and an important element that added to the widow population was child-marriage. In fact, two problems were associated with child-marriages. One was complications of early motherhood (at ages twelve, thirteen, and fourteen), such as abortions, miscarriages, and the deaths of young girls in childbirth. The other was that child-marriage increased the number of widows.[84] And it was for these reasons that such reformers as Iswara Chandra Vidyasagara began to argue against this practice in the 1850s.

Pre-puberty marriages of girls among most castes and classes of Hindus were commonly observed on various grounds: religion commanded it; if a girl was not married before the age of twelve, she might become unchaste bringing shame to the family honor; or a bridegroom might not be found if marriage was not celebrated whenever a suitable man was available. With these justifications widely accepted as true, girls between the ages of three and ten were not only married but, according to the custom, some were married to much older men[85] including middle-aged widowers[86]—men who died long before their younger wives, leaving them, according to the higher caste custom, widows for the rest of their lives. The result was that, around 1895, there were reportedly seven to ten million widows who did not exceed the age of ten.[87] With more castes practicing enforced widowhood, child-marriage and enforced widowhood became two parts of the same problem.

In 1860, Iswara Chandra Vidyasagara became instrumental in legislating a bill setting the age of consent for girls at ten, that is, "the age at which marriage could legally be consummated."[88] That decision of a male-dominated society to make wives of little girls of ten does not come as a surprise. By legislating such a law in order to abide by the wishes of the powerful patriarchy at the cost of much distress to girls, the colonial government also extricated itself from the problem of child-marriages.

Later, Katherine Mayo, an American journalist, centering her criticism of Hinduism largely on child-marriage, showed how the cruel custom killed or maimed little girls for life.[89] *The Pioneer*, in a long article, "The Hindu Marriage Question," basing its findings on police records, also showed the many cruelties of the custom.[90] While these criticisms may be interpreted as Western-centered, the fact remained that Hindu girls were married at an early age. And, though according to the custom, wives generally did not cohabitate with their husbands until puberty, the practice was, however, sometimes abused. And the legislation of 1860 only helped to worsen the lot of child-brides. Although, another law in 1891 was legislated prohibiting the marriage of girls under twelve,[91] it too had little success in fulfilling its desired object. As a result, the issue continued to be controversial and unresolved right through to the 1930s.[92]

Child-marriages, and child-widowhood were indeed causes for concern as an investigation in 1884 conducted by the Government in the North-Western Provinces and Oudh had shown that "infant widowhood was undoubtedly a source of much misery and immorality," but it added that the issue was not to the same extent as Mr. Malabari claimed.[93] The investigation had been conducted in response to Mr. Malabari's paper on "Infant Marriage" and "Enforced Widowhood" in India. But, while the Government of India requested an opinion on the two related subjects, child-marriage and enforced widowhood, it also advised the Government of the North-Western Provinces and Oudh to seek the opinion of "some orthodox Hindus of the old school, who would give their side of the question."[94] This was the same class of patriarchs whom the government was unwilling to "offend" by interfering in their religious and domestic affairs.

The report found that generally, Brahmans, Rajputs, Vaishyas, and others who claimed a similar descent, absolutely prohibited widow-remarriage and punished it with excommunication. Those lower peasant castes and classes who had *Panchayats* (a group or council of five convened to solve village disputes or, caste councils), on the other hand, practiced the custom "in defiance of the teaching and example of the enlightened ones" (the higher castes) and it was their "caste councils which gave sanction and validity to such marriages."[95] But many of those same lower castes/classes had begun to change their "defiance" to one of "compliance" when they thought of gaining "respectability" by emulation of those higher.

The report added that, of the total number of 38,053,394 Hindu people in the provinces recorded by the Census of 1872, the high castes/classes—the most wealthy, educated and high-born who practiced enforced widowhood—numbered 10,404,347. That meant that only a little over one-fourth of the Hindu population practiced the custom.[96] The report also compared the number of Hindu widows with that of the Muslims and found the difference not too great as Table 11 shows. The report noted further:

> Child marriage, besides its own peculiar evils, whatever they may be, is responsible for the existence of a large number of widows; and it is entire-

ly responsible for the worst form of widowhood, that of widows who have never been wives or mothers. But the bulk of Hindu women remain unmarried . . . because at 30 years of age she is an old woman, devoid of attraction and past the age of child bearing, and not likely to secure another husband. . . . Males remarry freely even in old age, but they do not choose second wives from among the grey widows of 30 and upwards.[97]

But while the report noted that child-marriage was responsible for the existence of a large number of widows and moral evils, it gave only a partial explanation of the Hindu situation. Comparing widows of the two religious groups, Hindus and Muslims, did Hindu widows no favor. The chances were that many of the Muslim widows would remarry, something that would not be true of many Hindu widows.

TABLE 11: Number of Hindu and Muslim Widows between the Ages of 9 and 14 in the North-Western Provinces and Oudh in 1882[98]

	Total Number of Female Population, Aged 9–14	Total Number of Widows	Percentage of Widow Population to Total Population
Hindus	1,820,134	21,417	1.2%
Muslims	293,109	2,113	0.7%

Second, old men and widowers not only avoided "grey widows," but they also never married little girl widows who had never been wives. They chose young unmarried girls. They were for these unjustifiable hardships and immoralities of widows that in 1848, Gopal Hari Deshmukh sent a memorandum to the government suggesting legislation to reform the custom of enforced widowhood.[99] In 1855, Iswara Chandra Vidyasagara, in an article, "Appeal on the Marriage of Hindu Widows," made a similar suggestion.[100] The result was a legalization of remarriage of Hindu widows in July of 1856 by Lord Canning.

There were, however, two problems with the law. Since it could not be enforced by penalty, it was not obeyed.[101] Furthermore, by specifying that upon remarriage, widows were to forfeit all the property inherited from their deceased husbands (as in Bengal), the law deprived widows of their civil rights.[102] In fact, what the colonial law said was that so long as a widow remained a widow and chose to have illicit intercourse, she could not be dispossessed of her husband's estate. But if she chose to have a lawful relationship by *marrying* the same man, she must then lose her property rights.[103] The law, therefore, by allowing a woman to choose between social stigma and poverty, changed nothing.

But why did orthodox Hindus oppose child-marriage and widow-remarriage reforms when it was obvious that the customs created vice, crimes and demoralization of females? Apart from such larger issues as "not wishing an alien power to interfere in religious" matters, either because of pride or nationalist political reasons,[104] patriarchy itself, in reaction to the "morals" of Western society, was also reformulating and strengthening its control over women, as was observed by James Samuelson in 1890. He noted that, although inferiority of native women was a factor,

> past history and the observation of the present also combine to make many of their [native] male relatives hesitate before consenting to their [women's] emancipation. The undisguised practice which obtained until recently amongst British Officers and Civil Servants, of keeping native concubines, is not forgotten; . . . but even amongst the English of the middle classes in India, there are many who are notoriously loose in their relations with the natives, and what is more startling to the latter, with each other's wives; whilst the English home journals, which are closely scanned by the enlightened natives, constantly give prominence to what are known as "*causes celebres*," reflecting little credit to English aristocracy.[105]

But, aside from the above factors, there is also reason to believe that there were different interest groups who for personal motivations opposed widow-remarriage. For them, religion mostly became a rationalization for the practice governing widowhood. The ideology that prohibited widows a regular diet, the use of ornaments, jewelry, decent clothes and a comfortable living, for instance, allowed relatives to strip widows of their property and belongings.[106] Many families almost entirely relied on free labor of widows who served as cooks, domestic servants, nursemaids, fieldhands and menials.[107] Then there is ample evidence to show that there were also many close male relatives who found helpless widows easy victims to satisfy their own lustful needs.[108] These men, who benefited from the plight of helpless widows, would have opposed any reform of enforced widowhood. And Brahman pundits (priests), too, after losing their income after Sati was abolished, derived a large part of their living from the offerings made by widows for the spiritual benefit of their deceased husbands.[109] It is doubtful if these men, the guardians of religion, would have been interested in widow-reform.

Then there was also a class of powerful "respectable Hindus" (high castes) whose interests conflicted with widow-remarriage because they kept young widows as concubines (see below). And finally, the colonial government itself, whose safety was assured by not "interfering in religious matters," was averse to legislating any laws to reform or abolish enforced widowhood. In fact, the notion that these customs were inherently rooted in religion, and therefore could not be abolished, was in a large part of the colonial government's own making. The government's often repeated assurances of "no interference" in such "religious" matters as "child-marriage and widow-remarriage" only reinforced orthodox opposition and its resistance to any reform.

Nonetheless, in May of 1876, the attention of the Government of India was again drawn to the issue of widows by Sir Madhava Rao. His concern revolved around the severe penalties of death or transportation for life imposed on widows who murdered their illegitimate infants. Because that crime was usually perpetrated by women under an overwhelming sense of shame and under extreme fear of social opinion, his proposal to the government was to limit their imprisonment to about seven years.[110] At his suggestion, the Government of India called for a report of all cases of widows murdering their infants that had occurred in British India within a given period of one to two years, together with the type of sentences awarded—execution or transportation for life.[111]

In 1879, the local governments and administrators reported that the working of the law against infanticide had no difficulties; therefore, no amendment was required. A total of 381 women charged with the murder of their illegitimate infants was reported from all British India. Three were executed, 152 were transported for life, and the remainder were imprisoned for various terms of years.[112]

In concurring with the opinion of the local governments, the Governor-General-in-Council noted that any relaxation of the law on the part of the government would indicate a disregard for human life. He also noted that *minor punishment of transportation* in proper cases of "infanticidal women" was preferable to imprisonment.[113] From imprisonment in India, he thought, a woman returned to the society a *tainted* outcast. But by transportation, she was placed in a new sphere, where, *if she again gave way to her instincts, there would be no inducement to kill her child*.[114]

It is noteworthy that both Rao and the Governor-General-in-Council merely expressed the entire prevailing attitude toward widows. First, no matter what the circumstances, rape or incest, it was a foregone conclusion that both the society and the law would find widows guilty on both counts, moral and legal. Second, the emphasis was on the punishment of widows and not on their education or reform, even though the Governor-General-in-Council had felt that the instincts of the "infanticidal widows might show themselves again." His solution to the problem was their transportation to the penal colonies. But it will be seen in Chapter 4 just what the sentence of transportation meant for women. Finally, a reform of the customs that made widows both victims and criminals was not even mentioned.

What the government's decision, in fact, did was to permit widows to continue committing crimes so long as their offenses were recorded by the police and they were punished appropriately. And although there were other proceedings—in 1885, 1893, 1899, 1900, 1901, and 1913—each, however, dealt with the "Procedures to be Observed in the Submission of the Records of Cases of Women Convicted of Murdering Their Infant Children."[115] Not a single proceeding was held to find a solution to the widow problem or of the infant-murders.

Nor were leniencies always shown to the widows in their punishments for their crimes as had been suggested by the Governor-General-in-Council. The opinion and attitude of a High Court Judge in Bombay Presidency represented the views of many when he refused to refer the case of a Vijaya Lakshmi, a Brahmin widow, to the government for mercy. In sentencing her to transportation for life, the judge "resolved to make an example of her case to widows who committed this heinous crime so often."[116] The focus of the colonial government remained on punishment as an example to deter crimes and as a means to enhance the "morality" of the colonial regime.

The administrators themselves had viewed the statement "twenty million suffering widows" as sensationalism because the number included widows of all religions, castes, and ages.[117] Their number and condition, they felt, were exaggerated by those who sought to glorify Christianity at the cost of Hinduism.[118] Although their view may have had some merits, the fact remained that the number of widows was astronomical. Nor was their large number the only issue, as already noted. Illicit sexuality of widows had become an issue of major proportion.

What was the result of the government's apathy in taking a firm stand against the widow problem and; why was it unable to deal effectively with the issue of widow-remarriage? Its own rationalization was that both those issues concerned religious and domestic related practices. They thus came under the "Non-Interference" clause of the Regulation of 1793; a clause that had given "emphatic pledges" that the colonial rule would leave religious and domestic customs of the people undisturbed.[119] That justification was, in fact, inconsistent with its policies on Sati and female (clan) infanticide. Sati and female infanticide were no less religious and/or domestic crimes, and yet they were abolished in spite of the Regulation of 1793.

Nor was the government's explanation that the "Hindu community seemed not to be prepared to accept restrictions" acceptable.[120] Hindu sentiment was not prepared to accept a ban on Sati either and it is doubtful if it would have ever accepted any reform without legislation supported by punitive measures.

The explanation that the British abolished those culturally important customs, including Sati, that seemed to present a challenge to the Raj while making the least impact on individual crime is plausible.[121] Sati was abolished in 1829, before the Mutiny, no doubt partly for humanitarian reasons. But Sati was overtly supported by the powerful conservative elements of the society, the Brahmans and the Rajputs. And, it can be safely concluded that its abolition supported by the force of legislation, was partly to demonstrate to them the strength and the supreme authority of the Raj. Mutiny, however, demonstrated two points to the rulers: one, that the power of the Raj could be challenged by the native conservative forces; and two, great caution had to be exercised in any interference with religious practices of the natives.[122] From 1857 onwards, then, it would seem that the British rulers became overly cautious as the security and the stability of the Raj became bound up with the conservative forces of the native patriarchy.

It is, therefore, not surprising that the issues of widow-remarriage and child-marriages should alone have continued to come under the clause "non-interference in domestic and religious" affairs of the Regulation of 1793. Strictly adhering to the non-interference policy in the interests of not offending orthodox patriarchy, meant that reforms affecting females had to be forestalled.

In fact the fears of the rulers were not totally unfounded as was evident in the acknowledgment of the Governor-General of the North-Western Provinces and Oudh when he "strongly deprecated" the passing of one particular bill in 1913. The bill was proposed by the Government of India to raise by legislation the age of consent of marriage for the protection of women and girls.[123] But the Governor-General of the provinces *noted an obvious danger in over-legislating on the subject of sexual morality.* Any such amendment, he felt, "would have converted into a grave penal offense the concubinage with deserted wives or widows of under eighteen," a practice he believed "*to be common and on the whole merciful.*"[124]

But the Governor-General saw no objection in passing one provision that called for the suppression of the symbolic marriages associated with religion that dedicated girls to temples. He noted that the practice was mainly associated with unclean and obscure forms of Hinduism which was immoral. But more importantly, the Governor-General felt that the custom could be "suppressed because there appeared *no danger* in so doing from most respectable Hindus."[125] What the Governor-General did not clarify, however, was the difference between the immorality of "unclean and obscure form of Hinduism" of the poorer people that dedicated girls to temples, and that of the "respectable Hindus" who kept young widows and other women in concubinage. For after all, both forms of immorality served one and the same purpose. Nor did the Governor-General explain why raising the age of marriage would not have been "moral" or more "merciful" to many little girls who either suffered from early motherhood or became widows before reaching their teen years only to become prostitutes or concubines of respectable Hindus.

The deciding factor for the Governor-General, obviously, lay not in whether a religion was clean or unclean, moral or immoral, merciful or unmerciful to women and girls, but rather in who presented a danger and a threat to the stability of the government.

It appears that the practice of concubinage was not uncommon in the provinces, as the Governor-General had himself observed. It was "fairly common and on the whole merciful." In fact, *The Hindi Pradeep* saw the system of concubinage as another stumbling block to any reform.[126] It held that an opposition to widow-remarriage came from that element of the society that took advantage of thousands of helpless widows for its own selfish purposes. Lamenting at the sad state of widows and the country, *The Hindi Pradeep* admonished those responsible for their degeneration in no uncertain terms (translation my own).[127]

The observation of *The Hindi Pradeep* was confirmed by a Sessions Judge in a case in 1908 when a man disposed his minor daughter to another to be his concubine. The judge noted: while the disposal of minor girls in that manner was *immoral*, it was not unlawful;[128] that it was common in the country for men to have concubines; and had the law intended to penalize in cases where girls were under sixteen, it would have been so stated as it had been done in the case of prostitution; finally, the judge concluded that it was for the legislature and not the courts to put an end to the practice.[129] By this ruling, concubinage had been judicially declared to be not contrary to law. And by the Governor-General's own rationalization that its existence was "more merciful to widows," the institution of concubinage was legitimized. Widows could either be put away in prisons or in concubinage in a society that was being modernized and moralized.

In any case, as the custom of enforced widowhood spread and the number of widows of all ages increased, so did "immoralities" and crimes. The difficulty with the ideological control mechanism that taught a widow to be chaste was that the control often lay not with the widows themselves but with the men around them, and usually their own relatives.[130] This pressure forced widows to "choose licentious ways in secrecy"[131] and to commit crimes of abortion and murder of newborn illegitimate infants. Such reports where a young widow who gave birth and then murdered her illegitimate infant as a result of her intrigue with her own father-in-law;"[132] or of the four reported illegitimate infant murders in Agra, noted in the 1911 police records as resulting from incestuous connections, were not rare.[133] Another and not an uncommon consequence of their dismal lives was the running away of widows into prostitution at an alarming rate.[134]

Some indication of the extent of crime committed by widows is shown by the following jail records of the North-Western Provinces and Oudh for different years in Table 12.

What these figures illustrate is that, when compared to the other categories of female criminals, the ratio of widow convicts was abnormally high. They figured approximately half of that of the married women (in general female population, widows represented a smaller percentage, one in five.) In the absence of police and court records, however, it is difficult to say just what percentage of widows were actually convicted for infanticide and what number may have been for any other crime. The exceptionally high figures during the scarcities and famine years of 1890, 1891, and 1897 may partly have been related to petty theft. But it seems fairly safe to conclude that the majority had been convicted for the murder of their illegitimate infants. Nor is this a comprehensive record of all the crimes committed by widows, as Mr. Malabari had noted:

> Direct evidence [in pregnancy] being nearly impossible in a suspected case, the policeman finds free scope for the exercise of mercy or cupidity. Yet, how many cases of infanticide do we hear of every month? And these are only exceptional cases that come to be known. The unknown ones may be twenty times more. There is a regular system of freemasonry maintained for the purpose—the removal of the widow in trouble on visits to distant relations or on pilgrimage—which baffles detection. When all attempts fail, the mother's health is ruined for life, or she dies with the babe unborn.[135]

Nor is it known how many pregnant widows may have been wickedly murdered by relatives to save family name. And, aside from widows as a social problem, attention was never paid to their psychological state. Overwhelming shame, extreme fear of being discovered, their "secretive behaviour," "denials,"[136] fear to disgrace family honor, and the endurance of pregnancy must have caused enough psychological trauma to drive many into committing suicide. It was under those same extreme pressure that many committed the unwarranted crime of infant murder.

According to the jail records, widow-murderesses came from different backgrounds, including high castes/classes as the following records show:

- A Brahmin widow buried her infant alive. The illegitimate birth was due to her relations with a Chamar; punishment not known.
- A Thakurain widow suffocated her illegitimate infant; she was transported for life.
- A Brahimini widow strangled her illegitimate child immediately after its birth; she was given ten years' rigorous imprisonment.

TABLE 12: Occupation of Female Convicts in the North-Western Provinces and Oudh Jails between 1878 and 1912 High Rate of Widow Convicts[137]

Occupation	\multicolumn{8}{c	}{Year}
	1878	1879	1880	1881	1882	1883	1884	1885
Married	9,521	970	951	804	811	1,764	1,436	1,335
Unmarried	564	29	52	42	50	112	80	95
Widows	-	541	442	482	487	581	70	628
Prostitutes	281	48	53	51	38	146	80	93

Occupation	\multicolumn{8}{c	}{Year}
	1886	1887	1888	1889	1890	1891	1892	1893
Married	1,519	1,699	1,789	2,056	2,081	2,627	1,067	1,747
Unmarried	72	89	86	130	80	87	65	60
Widows	785	711	672	834	894	967	828	711
Prostitutes	126	93	89	80	71	92	66	70

Occupation	\multicolumn{7}{c	}{Year}
	1897	1898	1901	1905	1907	1910	1912
Married	3,458	536	1,060	945	905	653	
Unmarried	180	13	83	29	30	20	
Widows	967	711	1,624	285	489	544	447
Prostitutes	92	70	77	20	80	58	47

Note: See Appendix B for religion and age.

- A Thakurain widow killed her illegitimate child immediately after its birth and buried it in a cotton field; she was sentenced to twelve months' rigorous imprisonment.
- One twenty-five-year-old Brahimini widow killed her illegitimate child directly after its birth and disposed of its body; she was sentenced to ten years' rigorous imprisonment.
- Another Brahimini widow gave birth to an illegitimate female child; its death was caused by foul play, and the woman was transported for life.
- A twenty-five-year-old Thakurain widow killed her illegitimate child a few days after its birth; she was transported for ten years.[138]

Nor were abortions and murder of illegitimate infants by widows in India committed for economic reasons as it may have been done in some other countries. They were committed to hide shame and to protect family name, consequently, the murder of illegitimate infants was carried out immediately at birth and, in desperation, widows sometimes employed diabolical means. One such case of infant murder occurred when a woman burned her illegitimate child in an earthen vessel in the middle of a large heap of cowdung.[139] She was hanged for her crime. Another woman thrust her infant in an earthen vessel and threw it away; a third woman cut her baby into two with a bill hook; a fourth killed it and buried it in her own home; a fifth forced a needle in the child's brain. And a sixth widow battered her child's head with a stone. Another widow murdered her child by severing the head from its body.[140]

These, then, were crimes and such other social "immoralities" as adultery, incest, polygamy, abortion, and prostitution, that so dismayed the reformers who had suggested that laws be passed permitting widows to remarry.

But the government's decision to refrain from interfering in the religious and domestic domains of the natives had a number of effects. By refusing to abolish the practices that affected almost one-half of the population, the rulers who were ushering in "modernization and moralization" on all fronts, became a party to the social vice, abortions, and murders of illegitimate-infants. Second, it denied protection to the widow and the female child, the two most helpless classes who critically required state protection. Third, it showed that just as the colonial rulers had done in economic development, so too they did in the judicial process: they marginalized women's interests. Fourth, by refusing to pass effective laws against child-marriage and for widow-remarriage, it permitted the Hindu social system to continue manufacturing women criminals for almost a century. And finally, the supreme irony of the government's non-intervention policy lay in the fact that it permitted its own laws to punish those very women it had helped to make criminals by denying them protection.

For the widow, however, her pregnancy and her crime of infant murder upon its birth, were only the beginnings of her tragic life. The rest was to follow as described here:

> It [the infant] is killed, and its remains are disposed of as best they can be. In this attempt great danger is incurred. The policeman considers it a piece of good fortune to discover such a body. He secures it and makes a list of young widows. . . . Many a widow, perfectly innocent, is laid hold of, taken to a police station, and marched off to a dispensary for medical examination. Some of them are declared innocent. The rest pay presents to the police, and recover their liberty from the clutches of the criminal law. . . . She may have no money . . . she is compelled to court a paramour. She is shunned by her relatives. It then becomes necessary for her to sell her body for the sake of bread.[141]

And those who were found guilty of their crimes began another sad and disgraceful phase of their lives as they faced either long term imprisonments or deportation to the penal colonies.

Meanwhile, all the social evils and crimes emanating from enforced widowhood continued to be associated with the "immoral behaviour" of widows as their wrongs and their woes. But lamentably, in holding the widows as the sole cause of all the sexual deviancies and crimes, the system that gave rise to those conditions was permitted to continue. And with it, the other half, the male population, that was equally if not more responsible in the creation of those social corruptions, illegitimate offsprings and crimes, was protected as well.

Even Gandhiji, the greatest reformer of all, writing in 1926, could say, "young girl widows . . . are a source of corruption and dangerous infection to society."[142] His solution to the widow-problem was the remarriage of child-widows. But he urged the grown-up widows to observe Satihood because a "Hindu widow was a treasure and Hinduism's gift to humanity."[143] And to him, a widow could prove her Satihood in realizing that the soul of her dead husband was not dead but lived on. Therefore, he advised widows never to think of remarriage but, with every breath that they breathed, they ought to shun all creature comforts and delights of the senses.[144]

It is not clear how old the grown-up widows had to be to follow Mahatama Gandhi's very noble though unrealistic advice. It is noteworthy, however, that while his solution for widows was living "Satihood," he, like most other patriarchs, neglected to reprimand that portion of the society that blatantly took sexual advantage of a helpless class of women. The society might have been better served had he taken man's sexual laxity into account as well and had recognized that not every living widow was a saint unto herself. And that she, too, as God's creature, was as subject to those same temptations as any man.

In any case, while abortion and murder of illegitimate infants were the most common crimes committed by desperate widows, there were times when they retaliated against the system and the society by other means. One such case in 1897, *Queen Empress vs. Tulsa,* showed[145] that Tulsa had administered poison to her own father, mother, and brother. The twenty-year-old woman, who was widowed before the consummation of her marriage, wished to live with a man of her own caste. Her wish was denied by her family on the grounds that widow-remarriage was forbidden in their caste. Tulsa then poisoned her family for her freedom. And in court, she admitted that she had committed the crime. Although her family survived and attempted to have her retract her statement of guilt, her sentence of transportation for life was upheld. The High Court observed that her action might have resulted in the deaths of three people.[146]

Tulsa's penal servitude for life serves to illustrate that for Hindu society a widow's life of a convict in the penal colony serving numberless male convicts was far more acceptable than her graceful remarriage and life with one man.

Another, and no less tragic life, was represented by one Jasoda.[147] A Brahaminee, widowed at six, Jasoda became a model of chastity, uprightness, and hard labor. She served as a cook, a housekeeper, a menial and, with each planting and harvesting season, a farm hand.[148] Yet because Jasoda was a widow, she was scorned by young and old alike, particularly by women. Angered by her young niece's spiteful insults one day, Jasoda threw a stone at the girl and unintentionally killed her. And, although the murder was accidental, widow Jasoda, at the age of seventeen, was hanged for her crime.[149]

Tulsa and Jasoda and many like them paid a high price for their crimes. But the system that gave birth to Tulsa and to Jasoda, and to many others like them, lived on. And so did the pride of those "respectable Hindus" who, under the false notion of their own "respectability" and family "sanctity," ignored the reality of the extent to which the condition of Hindu women had degenerated under colonial rule.

The objective of this chapter has been to illustrate how the issues of domestic violence and enforced widowhood were treated in colonial-patriarchal politics. When society accepted inferior and subservient position of women as a normalcy, it followed that it accepted abuse and battering of wives and women normal as well. Unfortunately, the colonial justice also failed to legislate for and to preside over subjects relating to women in a just manner. Finding no recourse to their abuses, those victims of oppression, like the women in economic distress, addressed their problems the only way they knew how, even if that meant committing crimes.

And, although there were many other interest groups that benefited from the institution of widowhood and opposed its abolition or reform, the ultimate decision for any change lay with the Government of India. And indeed, the Regulation of 1793 that specified "non-interference in domestic and religious affairs" of the natives benefited not women but the patriarchy. But, as it was, the process of state formation and the reconstitution of patriarchy proceeded at the same pace, each reinforcing the other against the interests of the poor and the women. In that process women's position deteriorated to new levels.

NOTES

1. Colonel Templeton in a paper read to the Parliamentary Committee for Women's Suffrage, 8 March, 1899; quoted in *Women of India*, p. 16; and various *Police and Jail Reports* of the North-Western Provinces and Oudh also reported the finding.
2. The figures are compiled from *Jail Reports* of different years. Statement No. 1, Judicial Criminal (for convicts only), "Showing the Number and Disposal of Convicts in the Jails."
3. Mary S. Hartman, *Victorian Murderesses. A True History of Thirteen Respectable French and English Women Accused of Unspeakable Crimes* (New York: Schocken Books, 1977), p. 5.
4. Sushil Chandra, *Sociology of Deviation in India* (Bombay, New York: Allied Publishers, 1967), pp. 197, 198.
5. Dharma Bhanu, *History and the Administration of the North-Western Provinces* (subsequently called the Agra Province), 1803–1858, p. 239.
6. *Statements Exhibiting the Material and Moral Progress and Condition of India for 1861-1862*, Appendix No. 4 (London), pp. 187–191. (Hereafter cited as *The Material and Moral Progress*.) This does not refer to the total number of female convicts in Port Blair, but only to those ninety-six inmates who were permitted to marry.
7. Home (Revenue and Agricultural) Department, *Report on the Administration of the Andaman and Nicobar Islands, and the Penal Settlements of Port Blair and the Nicobars, for the Year 1897*, Appendix VII, (Calcutta: 1879), p. 187.
8. In the United States it is only now that the "battered women syndrome"—women who have been both physically and psychologically beaten down by their mates and are suffering—is receiving attention. See, for example, "Battered Women Who Kill, Should They Receive Clemency?" *Glamour Magazine*, July 1990, 102.

    The subject, which is still controversial because there is as yet no scientific definition of the "battered woman syndrome," raises the argument that if physical and psychological abuse leads to a crime, should this abuse then be a justifiable plea of self-defense (*Glamour*, p. 102).
9. The figures are compiled from *Jail Reports* of different years. Statement No. 1, Judicial Criminal (for convicts only), "Showing the Number and Disposal of

Convicts in the Jails." There is a discrepancy in figures given in different reports.
10. Barbara D. Miller, *The Endangered Sex: Neglect of Female Children in Rural North India* (Ithaca: Cornell University Press, 1981), p. 15.
11. In the same manner as Sati, female infanticide and enforced widowhood were not practiced by all castes and classes.
12. Shoshee Chunder Dutt, *The Works of Shoshee Chunder Dutt, India: Past and Present, Historical and Miscellaneous*, vol. IV (London: Lovell and Reeve, 1884), p. 240 (hereafter cited as *India: Past and Present*); and D. E. Gimi, "Position of Women in India," quoted in *Papers on Indian Reform: The Women of India and What Can Be Done for Them* (Madras: The Christian Vernacular Education Society, 1888), p. 16.
13. S. C. Dutt, *India: Past and Present*, p. 240; P. Thomas, *Women and Marriage in India* (London: George Allen and Unwin, 1929), p. 27; and Shiva S. Dua, *Society and Culture in Northern India, 1850–1900*, pp. 4, 5.
14. S. C. Dutt, *India: Past and Present*, p. 244; and S. S. Dua, *Society and Culture in Northern India*, p. 11.
15. S. C. Dutt, *India: Past and Present*, p. 245; and P. Thomas, *Women and Marriage in India*, p. 27.
16. S. S. Dua, *Society and Culture in Northern India*, pp. 2, 4.
17. *Police Reports for 1888*, no. 1522A of 1889, p. 5.
18. Sir William Monier, "Speech from Zenana Missions," n. d., quoted in *Papers on Indian Reform*, p. 17; S. C. Dutt, *India: Past and Present*, p. 234; and M. Rangachari, *Papers on Indian Reform*, p. 17.
19. S. C. Dutt, *India: Past and Present*, p. 234.
20. *Police Reports for 1888*, no. 1522A of 1889, p. 5
21. Ibid.
22. Miss Leslie, *Woman's Work in the Indian Mission Field*, reprinted from the Report of the Calcutta Decennial Missionary Conference (Calcutta: Baptist Mission Press, 1883), p. 28.
23. S. S. Dua, *Society and Culture in Northern India*, p. 150.
24. Ibid.; Reverend William Buyers, quoted in *Papers on Indian Reform*, p. 11; and Bulloram Mullick, "Essays on the Hindu Family System," quoted in *Papers on Indian Reform*, p. 65.
25. William Crooke, *Things Indian: Being Discursive Notes on Various Subjects Connected with India* (London: John Murray, 1906), pp. 524, 525.
26. James Samuelson, *India, Past and Present: Historical, Social, and Political* (Ludgate Hill: Trubner and Co.), 1890; M. F. Billington, *Women in India* (London: Chapman and Hall, 1895); William Buyers, *Recollections of Northern India* (London: John Snow, Paternoster Row, 1848); and "The Women of India," *The Calcutta Review*, vol. 36 (January–June 1861): 315–343.
27. Ibid.
28. William Crooke, *Things India*, p. 522.
29. Ibid.
30. Cecil H. Walsh, "Deaf and Dumb," *Indian Village Crime* (London: Ernest Benn, 1929), p. 153; and M. F. Billington, *Women in India*, p. 123; *The Pioneer*, October 1890, p.2; and "The Women of India," pp. 315–343.
31. *Police Reports for 1914*, no. 352-VI-136-1915 of 1915, p. 8.
32. *Weekly Notes of the Cases Decided by the High Court of the North-Western Provinces for 1889*, Criminal Appeal No. 269, 4 July 1889, Queen-Empress v. Jia Lal, p. 181.

33. *The Pioneer*, 23 August 1890, p. 3.
34. Cecil Walsh, "Wifely Submission," *Indian Village Crime*, p. 163.
35. Ibid., p. 15.
36. Ibid.
37. *Police Reports for Year 1913*, no. 349/VI-159-1914 of 1914, p. 2.
38. Ibid.
39. *Indian Police Collection*; K. L. Gauba, *Famous Trials for Love and Murder* (Lahore: The Lion Press, 1945), pp. 191-196; and C. Walsh, "The False Confession," *Indian Village Crimes*, p. 189.
40. Ibid.
41. Under Hindu law, of the two offenses that could be punished with capital punishment, one was adultery. The adulteress was to be devoured by dogs, and the adulterer was to be burnt on an iron bed. H. R. Fink, "Crimes and Punishment under Hindu Law," *The Calcutta Review*, vol. 61 (1875): 31.
42. H. R. Fink, "Crimes and Punishments under Hindu Law," p. 31; and David G. Mandelbaum, *Society in India, Continuity and Change* (Berkeley, Los Angeles, London: University of California Press, 1970), p. 49. In the pre-colonial period, at least, the lower caste women's immoral behavior was handled by their *Panchayats*—a group or council of five that resolve village conflicts and disputes. D. Bhanu, *History and Administration of the North-Western Provinces*, p. 235; and D. G. Mandelbaum, *Society in India*, p. 305. (High-caste adulteresses were severely punished, as has been noted previously.) In cases among the lower castes where a husband failed to control his "morally erring wife," Panchayats sometimes took control in the belief that the whole caste was dishonored by one woman's immoral behavior. They sometimes imposed fines on husbands for not "controlling their wives," and at other times they threatened husbands with ostracization. C. H. Walsh, "The Caste Vengeance," *Indian Village Crimes*, p. 225.
43. D. G. Mandelbaum, *Society in India*, p. 49.
44. For instance, two wives were imprisoned on this one occasion; one was confined for forty-one days, and the other for forty-three days. *Jail Reports for 1890*, no. 3544/H-48 of 1890, p. 2; and *The Hindustan Kalakankar* (Pratabgarh), January, in *Confidential Selections*, 10 January 1890, p. 110.
45. H. R. Fink, "Crimes and Punishments under Hindu Law," p. 31; and D. G. Mandelbaum, *Society in India*, p. 49.
46. *The Pioneer*, 2 October 1890, p. 2; emphasis added.
47. Ibid., 7 October 1890, p. 3; emphasis added.
48. "Suicides in India," *The Pioneer*, 8 October 1890, p. 2. However, as noted by *The Pioneer*, death by drowning was mainly resorted to by women.
49. *The Pioneer*, 8 October 1890, p. 2.
50. Ibid.
51. Ibid.
52. Ibid.
53. *Annual Police Report of Oudh*, 1878, p. 11.
54. Ibid.
55. *Orders of the Government (Police) Department, North-Western Provinces and Oudh*, no. 652 of 1879, p. 19.
56. *Oudh Administration. (Criminal) Justice Report for the Year 1880*, no. 893 of 1881, p. 11.
57. Ibid.
58. *Police Reports for 1885*, no. 1686/11-14 of 1886, p. 190; and for 1896, no.

1686/11-14 of 1897, p. 18. This trend continued right through the period of this study. Sixty-nine women in 1912, and forty-two in 1913, perished with their children. *Police Reports of the United Provinces for 1913*, no. 349/VI-159-1914 of 1914, p. 1.
59. *Reports of Selected Cases Determined by the Court of Nizamut Adawlut in the North-Western Provinces, 1862-66* (Government Press), pp. 59–65.
60. Bhakat P. Mazumdar, *Socioeconomic History of Northern India, (1030-1194 A. D.)* (Calcutta: Firma K. L. Makhopadhyay, 1960), pp. 361, 366.
61. *Police Reports. Statements Showing the Number of Cases in Which Women Were Tried and Convicted for the Murder of Their Children by Criminal Courts.*
62. *Orders and the Resolution of the Government (Police) Department*, no. 764/VIII-54 of 1911, p. 6. It is interesting to compare these cases to those faced by Sir Charles Napier in Sind in the late eighteenth century. A vast number of Muslim women were found to be hanging themselves, apparently without any provocation. Sir Charles, however, discovered that the wives were being murdered by their husbands even for the most frivolous domestic affairs. But by reporting the murders as "suicides," the husbands always escaped. It was difficult to prove those murders because evidence, even when the facts were known to the entire village, was not forthcoming. Napier took an extreme measure. By making the villagers themselves responsible for the crime on the grounds of "conspiracy to withhold evidence," he successfully put an end to that practice. Edmund Charles Cox, *Police and Crime in India* (London: Stanley Paul and Company, n. d.), pp. 69, 259.
63. Ram Ahuja, *Crime Against Women* (Jaipur: Rawat Publications, 1987), p. 6.
64. *Jail Reports for 1902*, no. 190/H-48 or 1903, p. 2.
65. The Inspector-General of Prisons cited twenty-two cases where individuals were charged with attempts at suicide but, not one single person was convicted and sentenced to imprisonment in England. They were all discharged to Police Courts. Quoted in *Jail Reports for 1902*, no. 2 3190/H-48 of 1903, p. 2, from "Particulars of Insanity Contained in Table E, Appendix 24 of the 18th Report of the Commissioners of Prisons in England and Wales.

There was a clause in the Indian jail management rules permitting the removal of lunatic prisoners to asylums, but it seems it was very sparingly used. *Rules for the Management and Discipline of Prisoners in the North-Western Provinces* (Allahabad: Government Press, 1874), pp. 5, 29.
66. Ibid.
67. *Jail Reports for the Year 1902.* no. 3190/H-48 of 1903, p. 38.
68. Child-marriage, however, was believed to be prevalent among most castes and classes of Hindus. *General Department Notes and Orders on Infant Marriages and Enforced Widowhood in India, 1885*, File no.408/1885, p.1
69. Ibid., p. 208; S. S. Dua, *Society and Culture in Northern India*, pp. 5, 6; Pandita Ramabai Sarasvati, *The High-Caste Hindu Woman* (New Delhi: Inter-India Publications, 1984; rpt. Philadelphia, 1887), pp. 146, 147.
70. V. N. Datta, *Sati, Widow Burning in India* (New Delhi: Manohar, 1988), pp. 222, 223.
71. S. S. Dua, *Society and Culture in Northern India*, pp. 147 and 149.
72. Ibid., pp. 146, 147
73. Ibid.
74. D. B. Ragoonath Rao, quoted in W. W. Hunter, *The Hindu Child-Widow*, (Bombay: Voice of India Printing Press, 1887) pp. 117, 118; "The Hindu-Woman and the English Public," *The Pioneer*, 15 September 1890, p. 3; and Bulloram

Mullick, "Essays on the Hindu Family System," in *Papers on Indian Reform*, p. 119; and V. N. Datta, *Sati: Widow Burning in India*, p. 214.
75. *Government of India Legislative Assembly. Judicial (Civil) Department*, Debates Regarding the "Hindu Widows' Right of Maintenance Bill," Prog. no. 1(a), Serial no. 1 February, 1935.
76. Ibid., p. 3; and S. S. Dua, *Society and Culture in Northern India*, pp. 151, 152.
77. Government of India Legislative Assembly, "Hindu Widows' Right of Maintenance Bill," Prog. no. 1(a), Serial no. 1, 1935, p. 10.
78. V. N. Datta, *Sati: Widow Burning in India*, p. 185.
79. William W. Hunter, *The Hindu Child-Widow*, pp. 4, 13. Criminality of widows was not confined to India alone; for example, see R. W. Malcolmson, "Infanticide in the Eighteenth Century," *Crime in England, 1550–1800*, ed. J. S. Cockburn (Princeton: Princeton University Press, 1977), pp. 189–209; and J. M. Beattie, "The Criminality of Women in Eighteenth-Century England," *Journal of Social History*, 8.4 (1975): 84.
80. Reverend John Morrison, *New Ideas in India During the Nineteenth Century*, p. 36. In Great Britain, one in thirteen women was a widow during that period (ibid.).
81. Lata Mani, "Contentious Traditions: The Debate on Sati in Colonial India," in *Recasting Women: Essays in Colonial History*, p. 89.
82. *Notes and Orders. General Department*, "On Infant Marriages and Enforced Widowhood in India," 1885, File no. 408/1885, p. 1.
83. *Report of the Census of India*, 1901, pp. 442–443; and *Report of the Census of India*, 1921, vol. 1, part 1, p. 155.
84. *Notes and Orders. General Department*, File no. 408/1885, p.1; and Iswara Chandra Vidyasagara, "Appeal on the Marriage of Hindu Widows," quoted in *Papers on Indian Reform*, p. 117.
85. "The Women of India," *Calcutta Review*, (1861): 325–326. A law was enacted in 1860 which set the age of consent at ten years. *The Government of North-Western Provinces and Oudh. Judicial (Criminal) Department*, "Bill to Amend the Indian Penal Code and the Code of Criminal Procedure," February 1891, File no. 734B, p. 71.
86. Katherine Mayo, *Slaves of the Gods*, pp. 255, 257. Under Hindu law, co-habitation took place after the girl attained puberty, and in many instances the girl-bride lived with her parents until such time. If the husband died before that, then the bride continued to live with her parents as a widow for the rest of her life. These customs varied with different castes and classes.
87. *The Arya Darpan* (Shahjahanpur), February, in *Confidential Selections*, 10 February 1895, p. 245.
88. *Notes and Orders of the Government (General) Department, North-Western Provinces and Oudh*, "Infant Marriages and Enforced Widowhood in India," 1885, File no. 408/1885, p. 10.
89. K. Mayo, *Slaves of Gods*, p. 102; and Reverend John Morrison, *New Ideas in India*, p. 31.
90. *The Pioneer*, "The Hindu Marriage Question," 1890, p. 3.
91. H.L. Sarin, *The Child Marriage Restraint Act* (Calcutta: Eastern Law House, 1939), pp. 19, 22.
92. Ibid.
93. *Notes and Orders: General Department*, File 408/1885, p.1.
94. Ibid.
95. Ibid.

96. Ibid.
97. Ibid.
98. Ibid., p.3.
99. Pramila Dandavate, "Social Legislation and Women," in *Widows Abandoned and Destitute Women in India*, eds., P. Dandavate, R. Kumari, and M. Verghese (New Delhi: Radiant Publishers, 1989), p. 88.
100. Iswara Chandra Vidyasagara, "Appeal on the Marriage of Hindu Widows," quoted in *Papers on Indian Reform*, p. 117.
101. Ibid.
102. W. W. Hunter, *The Hindu Child Widow*, quoted in *Papers on Indian Reform*, p. 127; and S. S. Dua, *Society and Culture in Northern India*, p. 12.
103. W. W. Hunter, *Papers on Indian Reform*, p. 127.
104. Partha Chatterjee, "Colonialism, Nationalism, and Colonized Women: The Contest in India, the Women's Question in Tradition," *American Ethnologist*, vol. 16 no. 4 (1989): 823.
105. James Samuelson, *India, Past and Present: Historical, Social, and Political*, p. 59.
106. Bulloram Mullick, *Essays on the Hindu Family in Bengal* (Calcutta: W. Newman and Co., Limited, 1882), p. 65; and S. C. Dutt, *The Works of Shoshee Chunder Dutt*, p. 236.
107. S. S. Dua, *Society and Culture in Northern India*, pp. 116, 119.
108. Rao Bahadur C. H. Deshmukh, quoted in Mrs. Jenny Fuller, *The Wrongs of Indian Womanhood* (London and Edinburgh: Oliphant and Co., 1900), p. 62.
109. Ibid.
110. *Government of India Home (Revenue and Agriculture) Department. Judicial (Criminal)*, "Extract from the Proceedings of the Cases of Women Convicted of Murdering Their Infant Children," 27 September 1879, 3, File no. 142, January, 1901. (Hereafter cited as "Rules Regarding the Submission to Government of the Cases of Women Murdering Their Children," File no. 142.)
111. Ibid., p. 2.
112. Ibid., p. 4.
113. Ibid.; emphasis added.
114. Ibid.; emphasis added. In 1891, a group of widows signed and sent a petition to Queen Victoria asking her for an improvement in their condition. *The Khair Khwah-i-Panjab*, in *Confidential Selections*, 6 August 1891, p. 451.

    In 1902, another group of widows appealed to Lord Curzon asking that the remarriage of young widows whose husbands died before the consummation of their marriage be made compulsory by law. *The Arya Darpan* (Shahjahanpur), in *Confidential Selections* for the United Provinces only, 21, May 1902.

    And, of course, there were occasional individual women reformers such as Pandita Ramabai Sarasvati, who, herself a widow, wrote and traveled abroad, such as to Philadelphia, speaking and writing against child-marriage and advocating widow-remarriage. Pandita Ramabai, *The High-Caste Hindu Woman* (Philadelphia: 1888), p. 116.
115. *Procedure to be Observed in the Submission to Government of the Records of the Cases of Women Convicted of Murdering Their Infant Children*, (1888), File no. 142.
116. *The Pramod Sindhu*, (Amraoti), June 7, in *Confidential Selections*, 11 June 1881, p. 332; and *The Anwar-ul-Akhbar* (Lucknow), in *Confidential Selections*, 27 June, p. 384.
117. W. W. Hunter, *The Hindu Child Widow*, pp. 4, 13.
118. Colonel Temple, "The Women of India," in a paper read to the Parliamentary Committee for Women's Suffrage, 8 March 1899, p. 18.

119. W. W. Hunter, *The Hindu Child Widow*, 1887, p. 4.
120. Ibid., p. 33.
121. Sandria Freitag, "Collective Crime and Authority in North India," *Crime and Criminality in British India*, ed. Anand Yang, pp. 157, 158.
122. S. S. Dua, *Society and Culture in Northern India*, p.15. Ramabai had also concluded that so long as British Imperialism was served by Indian men, the rights of women would be subjugated. Quoted by Uma Chakravarti, "Whatever Happened to the Vedic Dasi?" in *Recasting Women*, p. 74.
123. *Government of the United Provinces Judicial (Criminal) Department*, "On a Proposal by the Government of India on Bills to Make Better Provision for the Protection of Women and Girls by Legislation," February 1913, File no. 970 of 1912, pp. 39-65.
124. Ibid.; emphasis added.
125. Ibid.; emphasis added.
126. *The Hindi Pradeep*, 1 August 1879, 11, no. 12, p. 7; author's translation.
127. Ibid.; my translation.
128. *Government of the United Provinces Judicial (Criminal) Department*, "On Sale of Young Girls in Garhwal," File no. 697 of 1908, 1908, p. 9; emphasis added.
129. *Judicial (Criminal) Department*, "On Sale of Young Girls in Garhwal," File no. 697 of 1908, p. 9.
130. D. B. Ragoonath Rao, quoted in W. W. Hunter, *The Hindu Child Widow*, pp. 117, 118.
131. Ibid.
132. *Police Reports for 1874*, 820A of 1875, p. 4.
133. *Police Department Resolution for 1913*, no. 1675, p.3.
134. I. C. Vidyasagar, quoted in *Papers on Indian Reform*, p. 117. Mohammadan prostitutes and dancing girls, known as *Tawaif*, also continually recruited their members from Hindu widows and discarded or deserted wives, but only after they embraced Islam. William Crooke, *The Tribes and Castes of North-Western India*, vol. IV (New Delhi: Cosmo Publications, 1975; repr. Calcutta: Office of Superintendent of Government Printing, 1896), pp. 361, 367.
135. B. M. Malabari, "Infant Marriage and Enforced Widowhood," quoted in *Notes and Orders of the Government (General) Department, North-Western Provinces and Oudh*, "On Infant Marriages and Enforced Widowhood in India," 1885, File no. 408/1885, p. 10. Although Mr. Malabari was a Parsee, he was one of the most ardent advocates of child-marriage and widow-remarriage reforms. He wrote many articles on the subject, made speeches and visited London expounding on the sufferings of widows.
136. For instance, Regina Schulte has observed the psychological trauma of women committing illegitimate infanticide in Bavaria. Regina Schulte, "Infanticide in Rural Bavaria in the Nineteenth Century," in *Interest and Emotion: Essays in the Study of Family and Kinship*, eds. Hans Medick and David Warren Sabean (London, New York: Cambridge University Press, 1984), pp. 77-99.
137. The figures are compiled from *Jail Reports, North-Western Provinces and Oudh, Statement No. 11. Judicial (Criminal)*, "Showing the Previous Occupation of Female Convicts Admitted into the Jails of the North-Western Provinces and Oudh" for the given years between 1878 and 1910.
138. Figures are compiled from *Police Reports* for different years. It was generally thought that women of respectable classes were "morally" pure; for instance, see M. F. Billington, *Women in India*, p. 122. In another case, when the

remarks of one Babu Chandi Charan Sen in *The Statesman*, stated that a large number of widows, including higher castes, lived immoral lives provoked much resentment, *The Statesman* found it necessary to qualify its position by saying, "while there can be no doubt that a very large number of this unfortunate class among the lower orders of society are unchaste, it is far from being amongst the higher classes of Hindu society where a standard of a very different order prevails." *The Statesman,* July 1888. Reprinted in *The Statesman: An Anthology*, comp. Niranjan Majumder (Calcutta and Delhi: 1975), p. 109.

139. *Judicial (Criminal) Department,* "Procedures to Be Observed in the Submission to the Government Cases of Women Convicted of Murdering Their Infant Children," January 1900, File no. 142, p. 7.
140. E. J. Kitts, *Serious Crime in an Indian Province*, p. 11; and various *Police Reports* have also recorded this.
141. B. M. Malabari, "Infant Marriage and Enforced Widowhood," quoted in *Notes and Orders*, "On Infant Marriages and Enforced Widowhood in India," File no. 408/1885, 1885, p. 10.
142. M. Gandhi, *Young India*, 26 August 1926, quoted in Dorothy K. Stein, "Women to Burn: Suttee as a Normative Institution," *Signs* (4 August 1978–Spring 1979): 263.
143. Ibid., p. 263.
144. Ibid.
145. *The Indian Law Reports*, Allahabad Series, vol. 18, 23 November 1897, p. 117.
146. Ibid., p. 117.
147. B. M. Croker, *Village Tales and Jungle Tragedies* (Piccadilly, London: Chatto and Windus, 1895), pp. 124, 145.
148. Ibid., pp. 4, 145.
149. Ibid.

3

The Colonial State: Modernization or Demoralization of Women?

The impact of the West on Indian civilization has brought about changes that are more fundamental in the case of women than of men. . . . The position of Indian women had been static for centuries, till western rulers, missionaries, Orientalists began to trouble the waters. First a tiny ripple disturbed the dead level, then fresh currents began to flow into the river. Now the whole surface is moving, breaking down the sluices and overflowing the ancient banks.[1]

This superficial Orientalist notion of the moralizing and civilizing missions of the West and its progressive effects on Indian women whose position had been mummified for centuries has been uncritically accepted for too long. While it might be true that the impact of Western influence on a handful of elite females had a more profound effect than on any other group under the colonial rule, it is also true that "progress" was not the only profound change to affect women. The fact is that there were two diverse and parallel revolutions occurring simultaneously for women. One was among the small minority at the top who "progressed" under the Raj, and the other was among the large majority of the lower castes and classes at the bottom whose position actually regressed with colonial impact.

In locating the penetration of colonial policies and their effects on women in three areas: the implementation of army cantonments in numerous cities and the recruitment of healthy peasant women for prostitution under the orders of the Imperial Government; the state's monopolization of the cultivation, manufacture, and the sale of alcoholic drinks; and the institution of emigration policies, this chapter demonstrates that far from its moralizing values, it was the colonial state itself that set the pattern for the "colonial culture against women" which had, in fact, an unprecedented demoralizing effect. And, while illustrating that women were more often victims of abuse, it at the same time, reiterates the stance that women criminals were often actually manufactured by the policies of the colonial rulers and high caste native patriarchy as the last two chapters have shown.

In the public/civilian domain of the society, the ideology of "respectability" was applied to divide women into two distinct groups, respectable and non-respectable classes, to serve colonial needs. While the concept of respectability/non-respectability was based on the Hindu social division of caste prejudices, the idea that women of "respectable classes" were governed by a "code of manners" and were "frail but appealing, intellectually inferior but morally superior" was not entirely foreign to the British Indian rulers themselves.[2] Consequently, in India, the ideologies of the two cultures that regarded the lower classes as "vulgar" collided and worsened the status of the subjugated female peasants. The policy of the colonial rule that honored the "purdah system" (seclusion), the "sanctity" and the "respectability" of the smaller but dominant higher caste/class females, on the other hand, was again, based on the same cautious approach of avoiding to offend and, thereby, alienate the powerful conservative forces.

That anxiety to avoid dishonoring high caste women was obvious in such fears as expressed by the Lieutenant-Governor of the North-Western Provinces and Oudh when he cautioned the Superintendent of the Police that "not unfrequently women of 'respectable morals' may be imprisoned, and, on being released, through the strangeness and helplessness of their friends, they may fall into a life of infamy."[3] Therefore, in making arrangements for their release from jails, "careful discretion according to the age and appearance, as well as the family *respectability*" was to be exercised in each case.[4] But whatever happened to the poor peasant women upon their release from the prisons was clearly not the concern of the Lieutenant-Governor.

The colonial rulers, however, also understood that the abuse of the peasant women would not arouse the sensibilities of the upper castes and classes; consequently, they found in their "assumed immorality" of the large majority of subordinate groups of women, a justification to ill-treat them. The "official" rationale that the lower castes and classes of women had no dignity to violate was applied by the state, alien soldiers, civilians, and the natives alike, to use and to abuse them at will.

In one Saharanpur rape case, for example, the four accused Europeans were acquitted of the crime even though the case was corroborated by medical examination and testified by witnesses. But worse yet, their acquittal was justified on the grounds that the women of the lower and poorer classes of the community "had no modesty to outrage."[5]

Assaults, violence, and harassment of the people in general[6] as well as ill-treatment and rapes of "the lower class of Hindoo women, who [were] naturally chaste, by British soldiers, with the sanction of their English rulers, and by the servants of the railway companies,"[7] were frequent and exceedingly glaring. The shameful behavior of the British soldiers in India was partly a consequence of the government's own policies.

The needed punitive measures to deter the soldier's crimes—which the colonial justice so readily imposed upon the poor and the women—were often not taken against the guilty soldiers which only encouraged their brutalities. Their merely token fines led the native population to suspect that the government was reluctant to give any severe form of punishment to the soldiers because it feared losing its Rs. 3,000 it had spent in importing them from England into India. Further, the authorities feared that any infliction of a severe punishment on a British soldier might create disaffection among the soldiers as a whole.[8] Their belief was not unfounded.

A law, in fact, had been passed in 1825 prohibiting magistrates "not only from punishing a British-European belonging to the forces, but also even from hearing evidence to the charge."[9] All any magistrate could do was to hand the offender to the military commanding officer, supposedly for a court-martial.[10] The grossly unjust law that prohibited legal redress against a large class of crime by the military personnel was addressed to by the Lieutenant-Governor of the provinces in 1852; the Advocate-General, however, ruled in favor of the law.[11] That meant that the ill-treatment, occasional murders of poor people, and debauching of women by British soldiers with the "sanction of the British rulers"[12] went unheeded as many vernacular papers continued to report frequently.

One 1888 case of a twelve-year-old girl, Bhoodia, presents a glaring violation of the morals of the subjugated women. Bhoodia was questioned by the magistrate in an open court if she ever had sexual intercourse.[13] But what was Bhoodia's crime? She had seen the accused, the man on trial, stealing, and she had been taken to the court as a witness.

The countercharge brought against the witness in favor of a thief by the magistrate himself—the guardian of the justice system (European in this case)— leaves one aghast at the colonial injustice towards women. But that was not all because, upon her denial, Bhoodia was subjected to a medical examination by a male doctor to verify that denial while her father and her brothers protested the insult in vain.[14] No woman, high caste or low, should have been humiliated in that manner nor her morals so unjustly and blatantly violated.

Bhoodia's case, however, received great attention because, as *The Statesman* observed, " the native papers would never have given the case more notice than they are in the habit of giving an ordinary 'coolie' case had not the depth and extent of the fears awakened in the native community" been so intense.[15]

As *The Statesman* noted, Bhoodia's case did receive much attention. But the concerns of the natives were aroused not because there was an anxiety for the low caste Bhoodia herself, but because of the perceived threat to women of higher castes/classes. Those "fears" were clarified by *The Bharat Bandhu* (Aligarh):

> If the Commander-in-Chief really means that respectable women also should be procured for European regiments, his orders are a disgrace and cannot be too strongly condemned. The protection of the chastity of their women is one of those great blessings of British rule for which the people are very thankful to Government and pray for the permanent establishment of that rule in this country.[16]

Whether the glaring discrepancy between the said "protection of the chastity" of the women and the actual treatment of the lower castes/classes of females was a pretended ignorance on the part of *The Bharat Bandhu* it is not known. However, it did depict the vast gap that existed between the attitudes towards the higher castes/classes and the lower castes/classes of women.

While the higher caste/class natives showed no more concern for the subaltern classes than did the alien rulers, it might, nonetheless, be noted that the Sedition Act of the colonial government had made the position of the native reporters quite precarious. In one rape case around the turn of the century, when an editor from Gujarat wrote: "Normally speaking, she was a sister to all of us. The Englishman, in a most cowardly manner destroyed the chastity of a respectable woman,"[17] he was sentenced to ten years' transportation. The presiding judge in that case observed, "I do not see what stronger language could be used by the writer for bringing into hatred or contempt or for the exciting disaffection towards the *Government established by law in British India.*"[18]

For the lower castes/classes of women, however, Bhoodia's was by no means an isolated case. It was reported that cases of ill-treatment of women like Bhoodia by the British magistrates were very frequent.[19]

But behind the violation, dishonor, and demoralization of the women were the orders of the very *Government established by law in British India*. The magistrates, in deliberately practicing illegal procedures, were only following those orders. A direction, which came to light in 1888, specified that the magistrates were expected "to provide healthy, young and handsome women procured from among the wives and daughters of peasants" for the "immoral" purposes of the British soldiers.[20] The rulers were fully aware of the Hindu custom of relatives disowning dishonored women; therefore, it deliberately used its legal system to dishonor innocent peasant women, such as Bhoodia. It then recruited them to serve its soldiers.[21] It was difficult to say how many unfortunate women, dishonored by the magistrates, had subsequently been turned out of the society and exposed to a life-long misery.[22]

The rules under the Contagious Diseases Act, designed to provide women to soldiers, had long been in force and were mainly framed to prevent the spread of venereal diseases among the British soldiers.[23] Consequently, there was always a large number of prostitutes living in the cantonment residences. In Cawnpore, there were 445 registered prostitutes in 1874, and in 1875 they numbered 389.[24] And with fourteen army cantonments in the North-Western Provinces and Oudh, located at Bareilly, Meerut, Agra, Cawnpore, Allahabad, Benares, Ranikhet, Naini Tal, Chakrata, Roorkee, Moradabad, Shahjahanpur, Muttra, and Jhansi, it is not known how many females were forced into prostitution by the government's policy.

The prostitutes living in the cities who were visited by the soldiers were also subject to the cantonment regulations. The failure to register and to report for medical examinations were crimes resulting in their arrests, fines, and imprisonments.[25]

And according to the government reports, other than the resident prostitutes, there was always a large influx of the lowest classes of prostitutes to serve the soldiers.[26] That should not come as a surprise knowing that the large class of starving homeless women, abandoned women, and widows was also a creation of colonialism and expanding capitalism; they found prostitution the only means of subsistence. And the establishment of fourteen cantonment-brothels and the recruitment of peasant women into prostitution was tantamount to giving an open invitation to poor women to earn a living.

On the entire question of prostitution and disease, however, the colonial government's concern remained limited to the control and punishment of prostitutes even though the method of controlling disease, as the Governor-General of the provinces himself saw, was "to put pressure on the men rather than on the women."[27] But applying pressure on the soldiers was against the governments's policy and, ironically, the only "immoral" party in that triangular affair—among the government, the soldiers, and the women—was continually perceived to be the women only. They were labeled as "absolutely without morality"[28] by none other than the party that corrupted them. And therein lay the crucial point—the difference between the prostitutes practicing their profession willfully, and prostitution thrust upon innocent women by the government through its legal machinery. But the government's role as the procurer of prostitutes was conveniently disregarded by the colonial history-makers. Thus, the record of its own "morality" was left unblemished as it remained supremely convinced of its own "moralizing" and "civilizing" missions.

However, when questions arose in Parliament in 1888 regarding the provision of women for European soldiers for "immoral purposes," the Government of India admitted that such arrangements had been made and that it felt "ashamed" of those arrangements.[29] And to put a stop to those practices, a provision was passed by the Parliament on June 5, 1888, repealing the Contagious Diseases Act. Referring to that repeal, *The Bharat Bandhu* (Aligarh) expressed the gratitude of the whole native population to Mr. MacLaren, who had been instrumental in the repeal of the Act.[30] But evidently the expression of that "gratitude of the whole native population" to the British Government for repealing its own disgraceful arrangements was somewhat premature because, although the Act was repealed, the practice continued with the approval of the government itself. It took two American ladies, five years later, in 1893, to expose the continuance of the vice in Indian cantonments. And it was due to their efforts only that the practice was finally repealed.[31]

The general uncontrolled behavior of the soldiers in India was also partially related to the state of their alcoholism. It was reported that the consumption of spirits in the British Army was a grave problem. And it was that condition of drunkenness that caused nine-tenths of their crimes.[32] But neither intoxication nor looseness of character was confined to the British soldiers alone. Occasional accounts suggest that intoxication and crime were quite prevalent among English civilians as well, and in most such cases, native women were their victims.[33] Whether the monopoly of the government to manufacture liquor indirectly encouraged alcoholism among its own people and army, as it did among the natives, is not clear.

What the evidence overwhelmingly supports, however, is that the effect of the government's monopoly of the cultivation, distilling, and the vending of liquors encouraged alcoholism among the natives, and once again, women were the victims of the government's policy. Alcoholism among men not only intensified the poverty of the lower strata of the society, but also induced crimes as it had done among the British soldiers. Such newer methods to maximize excise revenue as the advance payment to the cultivators, the farm-out system, and the granting of licenses, to "respectable" persons[34] provided incentives for the production, distribution, and consumption of alcohol. The distribution method and the easy credit system made intoxicants readily accessible, which encouraged alcoholism.

An enormous number of shops, 4,341 in all, were opened in the provinces for the sale of intoxicants during the years 1873–1874 alone.[35] This number in itself proves that the business of consumption of liquor was brisk in the provinces. Yet the Lieutenant-Governor found no evidence to support the contention that the government rules for vending alcohol had stimulated consumption. But then, no government official was expected to find the government's own practices detrimental to public health and morals, especially when the excise revenue derived from that source was second in importance only to the revenue from land.[36]

The case of such castes as that of the Bhangis, or the sweepers, the lowest of all the serving castes, who were notoriously addicted to drinking, also confirms the prevalence of alcoholism. Their known behavior of thieving, of treating their own women violently, and sending their daughters out to earn money as prostitutes when other means failed were direct results of their alcoholism.[37] The Ahirs, or the cow-herders, were also famed for drunkenness. And when "20,000 to 30,000 strong Ahirs," and certain other castes numbering another 10,000, were forbidden by their castes the use of intoxicating liquor, the loss was quickly felt at the *toddy* (intoxicating beverage made from the sap of palm) and liquor shops.[38]

But while there is no official record of women drinking, there is evidence of their plight because of alcoholism of their husbands. One incidence recorded by Mahant Kesho Ram Roy, an activist in the temperance movement in the Benares area, represents the condition of many. During his lecture to the impoverished Kolee (weaver) caste of Agra, he noted:

> seven Kolee women (who were all the while standing and hearing my lecture very patiently) came forward and fell prostrate before me, crying and bitterly lamenting the misfortunes which the grog-sellers' demand had brought upon them. They said that all their ornaments and even their utensils had been sold to liquidate the grog-sellers' demand. *The grog-sellers had robbed them right and left by supplying their husbands with liquor on credit.* [39]

The question of whether alcohol consumption was customary in the precolonial period is not the issue here, although it had been observed that Hindus were a sober nation who indulged in alcohol chiefly during their festivals.[40] The issue here is that drunkenness and crime were both on the increase because of easy access to toddy[41] and liquor shops. It was the newer innovations of the government in the production and distribution of the alcoholic drinks that led to a great increase in its consumption and a corresponding increase in the crime rate.[42] The easier method of selling liquor and toddy on credit did nothing less than to make addicts of the peasants and, consequently, bring much suffering to their entire families.

The growing indulgence in alcoholism and crime among the natives was also deplored by the personnel of the courts of justice and of the excise department. They did not hesitate to attribute that degradation where it existed—as in Ahmedabad, Delhi, Agra, Lucknow, Benares and other places—to alcoholism, rather than to any change in the generally temperate habits of the people.[43]

Another and more vigorous agitation against the government's excise policy, however, was represented by the organizers of the late nineteenth-century temperance movement.[44] It was due to the efforts of the Temperance Society that the Congress Party in 1893 resolved to call upon the

Government of India to "suppress the common sale of alcohol, opium, hemp drugs, and other intoxicants, and so cease to derive any portion of revenues from the 'vice, degradation, and misery of the people.'"[45]

The third policy of the government to degrade women was the emigration policy which actually became a double-edged sword for them: On the one hand was their and their children's abandonment by their emigrating husbands, as discussed in Chapter 1; on the other hand were the foul means employed by the recruiters to recruit them.

Kidnapping of females in the provinces was not new. However, the usual motives prompting the crime were limited either to recruiting for marriage or for prostitution.[46] But under colonialism, just as there was a new demand for women in the penal colonies and in the cantonments, so also there was a requirement for women in the developing colonies abroad, and in Punjab, where the government was engaged in canal construction.[47] And as their need grew with the emigration policy, so did their abductions, kidnappings, and seductions of girls and young married women from their parents and husbands over a large geographical area. In fact, kidnapping as a profession was so vigorously pursued that it formed a basis for a special report.[48] In 1881, for instance, 180 persons were convicted of that crime.[49] And during the first decade of the twentieth century, a scarcity of marriageable young women in Punjab made the supplying of women so lucrative that within a few months over one hundred Hindu and Muslim girls were kidnapped.[50]

Although the colonial state was supposedly neutral in the migration system, it was, in fact, the state itself that regulated and legislated policies to maintain labor migration.[51] However, the difficulty with emigration system was that, while the government licensed recruiters, it neither scrutinized their character nor properly supervised their activities. The result was that, because it was difficult to recruit the specified number of females, foul methods were regularly employed to obtain women of all ages.[52]

The emigration depots where emigrants were confined for external emigration were not supervised either. Consequently, the depots became another place where women were victimized. Kidnapped females were often threatened by violence to keep silent.[53] And frequently, women were not only decoyed to the emigration depots and illegally detained but, when once there, they were also raped.[54]

Since there was little control over the activities of the recruiters, and also because when once enticed away from home many were abandoned by their relatives, no accurate records were kept of the number of women recruited and/or abducted and abused. Some estimates report that barely 1–2 percent of the criminal offenses perpetrated inside the depots came to light.[55]

Nor was the abuse of women, because of the emigration policy, confined within India. Their lives in colonies were far more disgraceful. The government's practice of discouraging family units to emigrate as a whole, and the specification that forty women emigrate with every one hundred men resulted in the worst types of vice among the Indian emigrants.[56]

Another impact of the lack of control of the emigration in the North-Western Provinces and Oudh was that it directly or indirectly induced networks of kidnapping, those in which women were sold for any use. An example of the trade that developed between Mirzapur (The United Provinces) and Amritsar (Punjab), the two largest carpet manufacturing centers during the first decades of the twentieth century, is only one illustration. An ingenious scheme was devised whereby girls being sent for sale from Mirzapur to Amritsar were labeled as "carpets." A system of distinguishing girls for various purposes based on their beauty was also devised. "Red carpets" denoted beautiful and well-favored girls who were sold for as much as 10,000 rupees. "Blue carpets" were less favored, and "black carpets" generally found their way into the houses of "ill-fame."[57]

Accounts of the cantonments, the spread of the use of intoxicants, and of the emigration system are given here insofar as they demonstrate how women were exploited and disgraced in so many ways by the colonial rulers. Their history here is by no means full and complete. The demoralization of women was no where better illustrated than in their recruitment to serve British soldiers and in their emigration policy to serve men and help develop colonies that brought immense benefits to the Imperial Government. And, wherever the rulers exported Indian laborers/prisoners, they exported the ideology of "immorality" of the subjugated women to serve their purpose. In the Fiji Islands, for instance, the very government and the white planters who wanted single male laborers only, but also specified the emigration of forty single women to every one hundred men, found a cause to label Indian laborers as an "immoral lot."[58]

Aside from the deliberate policies of the colonial rulers—cantonment regulations, manufacture and sale of intoxicants, and the emigration system—the impact of colonial rule also radically transformed the villages. And the influence of such Western ideals as professionalism, individualism, and capitalism did not always have positive results. The change and decline of the ancient Hindu systems, particularly of the property laws—from communal holdings to individual holdings—brought property disputes, landlessness, and family disintegration. Ultimately, the domestic relations themselves began to undergo a revolution that was too "appalling to contemplate."[59] That revolution was "not confined to this or that sect, this caste or that caste, but to almost every household, Brahmin or Sudra."[60]

This social revolution might in part also explain the many cruel murders of women during this period. Disintegration of the family and of domestic lives began to affect the code that regulated sexual and gender relations. Some women found that adultery and prostitution in cantonments, for example, allowed them to survive and to have some degree of independence from the patriarchal hold. But for the patriarchy, the last thing to be surrendered in any transition period would have been the code that governed a man's relationship with his wife. Therefore, it would appear that, in an effort to control women's changing behavior, punishments for deviancies became more frequent and more brutal.

Accounts of murder—such as of a headless body of an unidentified woman bearing no marks of violence found in a well near Jhansi;[61] a dead body of a woman floating in the large tank along the railway station road; a woman's corpse found in a well partially filled with rubbish in Shahganj; or a female body found on the Dariabad Road[62]—were not rare. What is more troubling is that brutal murders of unknown or unidentified women went unexplained; the chances were that their murders were not even investigated.

These murders and many abuses of women come as a shock because of, as Maria Mies has observed, "the cherished view that India was a country where women were more respected than in many parts of the world."[63] It is possible that just as exploitation of women was a part of colonialism, so too, their abuses and murders signified the changing values and uncertainties of the period. While many innovations had changed and were changing village relationships, the mentality and the attitude of the people themselves had not changed. The co-mingling of the old values, beliefs, and superstitious practices with the new forces marked the period with great instability.

The major focus of this chapter has been to illustrate the blatant and politically motivated abuses of the subjugated classes of women in civilian life by the colonial rulers under the guise of the ideology of "respectability and non-respectability." The needs of the developing state, the consolidation of its power, protection, and the stability of the rule, required the appeasement of the superior castes and classes. A part of that appeasement policy was that "respect" be accorded to their women. Thus, the "divide and rule" policy that applied to women was simply another means of fulfilling the colonial needs. The Contagious Diseases Act, the monopolization of the liquor industry, and the emigration policy each had similar effects of demoralizing and abusing the same class of women.

Second, though the whole surface was moving under the nineteenth-century colonial and Western influences, it was not always moving in the right direction for a large majority of the women. Nor was it breaking down any "sluices" for them. (It could be argued that it was the twentieth-century wars, mass media communication, and the rapid transit system—all Western influences—that has had a far greater impact on the lives of all classes of women.) On the contrary, the imperatives of the colonial rule that divided women brought many disguised forms of abuse and exploitation of the lower castes/classes of women. Though they have been reformulated, abuses have continued in the independence period.

Undeniably, the Hindu social system itself, to some extent, abetted the colonial policies and provided another underlying influence of violence against women. The concern of the middle class natives for "respectable" classes of women at the cost of all the others, a distinction that was used by the colonial rulers to develop discriminating policies for the Indian females, brought untold hardship and suffering to the lower castes/classes of women.

"Respectability" had its advantages. And it was for that reason that, when the Sarda Committee was seeking evidence, Ram Chandra advised the village heads to "demand similar status for the women of the lower castes as enjoyed by the high caste women."[64] This, as he saw it, was a major step towards gaining that respectability. The enforcement of a uniform but strict code of sexual morality by the peasants themselves, however, would have to be the first step.[65]

However, for subjugated women, the middle-class notions of sanctity and morality might have brought respectability but, with those ideas, they would have lost their freedom. In any case, the decision to adopt a code of sexual morality to bring respectability was not always in the power of the lower castes and classes of women themselves. That power lay partially with the men of the dominant castes and classes around them.

Finally, when expounding the notion that the impact of colonial rule had profound changes for the better for Indian women, the caste/class of women who may have benefited from that impact must be specified. For, as this study shows, colonialism brought untold miseries to the large majority of laboring-class women whose position actually deteriorated and who are still struggling to share in the progress enjoyed by the higher castes and classes.

NOTES

1. Mrs. H. Gray, "The Progress of Women," *Modern India and the West*, pp. 445, 483. For example, in the 1890s, only 21 in 10,000 of the females were educated. W. Crooke, *The North-Western Provinces of India: Their History, Ethnology, and Administration* (London: Methuen and Co., 1897), p. 153.
2. Mary S. Hartman, *Victorian Murderesses*. (Schocken Books, 1977), p. 2.
3. *Proceedings of the Judicial (Criminal) Department. On Entertainment of the Matrons and Female Warders on the Prison Staff Jails in Which Female Prisoners Are Confined.* Resolution No. 537A, April 3, 1873, in Proceedings for February, 1888. Judicial (Criminal) Department, N.-W.P. and Oudh. File No. 62B, p. 8.

4. Ibid., p. 8; emphasis added.
5. *The Dabdaba-i-Qaisari* (Bareilly), January 13, in *Confidential Selections*, January 18, 1883, p. 63; and numerous other vernacular papers continued to lodge complaints against the behavior of the British soldiers.
6. *The Dabdaba-i-Qaisari* (Bareilly) January 13, in *Confidential Selections,* January, 18, 1883, p. 63. Samuelson's observations on the "loose" behavior of the middle class English in India was much closer to the truth than was often known. Their heavy addiction to intoxicants was the other side of the "notoriously loose" character which did not impress the natives at all (J. Samuelson, *India, Past and Present,* p. 5).
7. J. Samuelson, *India, Past and Present,* p. 5.
8. *Dabdaba-i-Qaisari,* January 13, in *Confidential Selections,* January 18, 1883, p. 83.
9. Dharma Bhanu, *History and Administration of the North-Western Provinces,* p. 256.
10. Ibid.
11. Ibid.
12. J. Samuelson, *India, Past and Present,* p. 5.
13. *The Statesman and Friend of India.* July 12, 1888, p. 3; and *The Hindustan* (Kalakankar), August 1, in *Confidential Selections,* August 7, 1888.
14. Ibid., p. 3.
15. Ibid.
16. *The Bharat Bandhu* (Aligarh), July 13, in *Confidential Selections,* July 24, 1888, p. 459.
17. Iqbal N. Singh, *The Andaman Story.* (New Delhi: Vikas Publishing House Pvt. Ltd.), p. 189.
18. Ibid.; emphasis added.
19. *The Hindustan,* (Kalakankar), August 2, in *Confidential Selections,* August 7, 1888, p. 499.
20. *The Prayag Samachar* (Allahabad), June 18, in *Confidential Selections,* June 19, 1888, p. 382. Quoted from an article from a pamphlet called "Is India to Perish from the Sin of English Men?" It was published by Mr. Dyer, the editor of the *London Sentinel.* It gave the substance of the system of procuring women for European soldiers for immoral purposes.
21. The Hindustan (Kalakankar), August 2, in *Confidential Selections,* August 7, 1888, p. 499.
22. Ibid.
23. *Proceedings of the Home (Sanitary) Department* in Lock Hospital Reports of the North-Western Provinces for the year 1875. Progress Nos. 19–21. November 1876, p. 6. (Cited as Lock Hospital Reports, 1876, hereafter.) Proper registers were kept on the prostitutes with their names, disease, the number of times they reported for medical examination, punishments awarded for non-attendance, and hospital records, etc. The prostitutes who lived in cities opposed registration and they frequently employed lawyers, with success, to defend their rights. *Lock Hospital Report from Allahabad,* p. 2.

There were also colonies of foreign prostitutes in almost all cantonments. They came mostly from Japan, China and, some from Austria. The keepers of the brothels were usually Parsees. Many women, European and Asiatic, including some from Tripoli and Turkey, also found their way to Lucknow from time to time. It appears they went there on their own. *Proceedings of the Government, United Provinces Judicial (Criminal) Department. File Heading: Bill to Suppress the Importation of Foreign Women for Prostitution.* File No. 948/1912, p. 3.

And, apparently, modern white slave trade was also on the rise as the police of the United Provinces began an active campaign against traffickers in women. Augustus Somerville, *Crime and Religious Beliefs in India,* (Calcutta: W. Newman and Co. Ltd., 1929), p. 2.
24. *Lock Hospital Reports from Cawnpore,* 1876, p. 6.
25. *Lock Hospital Reports,* Working of the Lock Hospitals, 1876, p. 2.
26. *Lock Hospital Report from Bareilly,* November, 1876, p. 3.
27. From the Officiating Secretary to the Government of the N.-W.P. to the Officiating Secretary to the Government of India, quoted in the *Lock Hospital Reports,* 1876, Appendix, p. 57.
28. *The Bharat Bandhu* (Aligarh). July 13, in *Confidential Selections,* July 24, 1888, p. 459.
29. *The Mihr-i-Nimroz* (Bijnor). June 28, in *Confidential Selections,* June 28, 1888, p. 417.
30. *The Bharat Bandhu* (Aligarh). July 13, p. 459.
31. *The Cawnpore Gazette,* September 25, in *Confidential Selections,* October 4, 1893, p. 405.
32. Frederick Thesiger, "A Plea for the British Soldier in India," *Agra Soldiers' Total Abstinence Association.* (London: William Tweedie, 337 Strand, 1876), p. 5.
33. Ibid.; J. Samuelson, *India, Past and Present* ; and vernacular papers.
34. *Administration Report of the Government of India.* 1873-1874. Part 3. (N.-W.P. Record Department, Allahabad: 1875), p. 218. (IOL V/10/137)
35. Ibid., p. 218.
36. David Hardiman, "From Custom to Crime: The Politics of Drinking in Colonial South Gujarat," *Subaltern Studies IV. Writings on South Asian History and Society.* Guha Ranjit, ed. (Delhi: Oxford University Press, 1985), p. 165. In 1930–1931, the United Provinces' revenue was 65 percent from land and 12 percent from excise. *The Indian Year Book.* (Bombay, 1931), quoted by Hardiman, David, ibid, p. 165.
37. John C. Nesfield, *Brief View of the Caste System of the North-Western Provinces and Oudh.* (Allahabad Government Press, 1885), pp. 40–41.
38. Report of the Temperance Society in Benares, in J. Samuelson, *India, Past and Present,* 1890, p. 59. The movement was "organized, patronized, and instructed" by English philanthropists and missionaries. And it was through the suggestion of philanthropist William S. Caine, a Liberal member of Parliament who had many years of experience in temperance work in England, that alcoholism from a social and moral problem, became a political issue as well. It was also through his efforts that the Congress, the Brahmo Samaj, the Arya Samaj, and Christian organizations were all brought together in that agitation movement. Lucy Carroll, "The Temperance Movement in India: Politics and Social Reform," *Modern Asian Studies,* October 3, 1976, pp. 417–447.
39. Mahant Kesho Ram Roy, in Lucy Carroll, "The Temperance Movement in India pp. 417–447; emphasis added.
40. J. Samuelson, *India, Past and Present,* p. 59.
41. *Police Reports for 1911.* No. 263/V1-99, 1912 of 1912, p. 9.
42. J. Samuelson, *India, Past and Present,* 1890, p. 218.
43. Ibid., p. 253.
44. Ibid.; and Leslie, Miss, a paper presented to the *Woman's Work in the Indian Mission Field.* Reprinted from the Report of the Calcutta Decennial Missionary Conference (J. W. Thomas, Calcutta, Baptist Mission Press, 1883), p. 29. (Cited hereafter as Woman's Work in the Indian Mission Field.)

45. Lucy Carroll, "The Temperance Movement in India," pp. 417–447.
46. Hollins in *Indian Police Collection*.
47. Ibid.
48. *Police Reports for 1887*, No. 828A of 1888, p. 6. For instance in 1880, 157 persons were sentenced for this offense to an average term of five months each.
49. *Criminal Statements of the N.-W.P.* for the Calendar Year 1881. With Prefatory Note, p. 5: and various Police Reports.
50. Hollins in *Indian Police Collection*.
51. Gail Omvedt, "Migration in Colonial India: The Articulation of Feudalism and Capitalism by the Colonial State," *The Journal of Peasant Studies*, vol. 7, no. 2, January 1980, pp. 204–206.
52. Hollins in *Indian Police Collection*.
53. *The Ridz-ul-Akhbar* (Gorakhpur), January 8, in *Confidential Selections*, January 16, 1895, p. 25.
54. *The Prayag Samachar* (Allahabad), May 2, in *Confidential Selections*, May 6, 1901, p. 123.
55. Ibid., p. 123.
56. As it was pointed out in the case of Fiji, C. F. Andrews and W. W. Pearson, *The Report on Indentured Labour in Fiji* (Calcutta, 1916), p. 20; and Florence Garnham, *Report on Social and Moral Conditions of Fiji Indians*, n.p., 1916. The report was prepared for the Women's Organizations in Australia and New Zealand. Quoted in Priyam B. Singh, *Fiji's Indentured Labourers, 1864–1920*, pp. 98, 100.
57. Augustus Somerville, *Crime and Religious Beliefs in India* (Calcutta: W. Newman and Co. Ltd., 1929), pp. 6 and 7.
58. H. H. Thiele, "Agriculture in Fiji," *Proceedings of Royal Colonial Institute*. XXI, 1889–1890 (London), pp. 374–382.
59. Bulloram Mullick, *Essays on Hindu Family in Bengal*, p. 86.
60. Ibid., p. 12. Note: The murder of prostitutes, which was also not infrequent, was committed partially because of their profession and partially for sexual jealousies. Occasionally, their visiting customers also murdered them for theft. But such gruesome means employed to murder them, as was the case of an aged prostitute in Budaun whose throat was cut, stomach ripped open, and body thrust into a thatched hut which was then set on fire, portray a remarkable form of cruelty (*Police Reports for 1914*. No. 352-V1-136, 1915 of 1915, p. 6).

    Another extraordinary series of murders of prostitutes occurred in 1905 in Meerut, Hardwar, Benares, Muttra and other sacred places in the United Provinces at the time of full moon when victims' throats were cut and holes dug to catch the blood (*Police Reports for 1906*. No. 354/1-249-07 of 1907, p. 6; and Hollin's Report, *Indian Police Collection*).
61. *The Prayag Samachar* (Allahabad), December 13, in *Confidential Selections*, December 19, 1894, p. 25.
62. *The Prayag Samachar* (Allahabad), March 19, in *Confidential Selections*, 1896, p. 55.
63. Maria Mies, *The Lace Makers of Narsapur*, p. 1.
64. Kapil Kumar, "Rural Women in Oudh 1917–47: Baba Ram Chandra and the Women Question." *Recasting Women. Essays in Indian Colonial History*, p. 337.
65. Ibid., p. 19.

4

Colonial Justice, the Penal System, and Women Criminals

The argument that the British Indian administration facilitated judicial reform and that it abolished ancient forms of barbarous punishments,[1] cannot be denied. Nor can the eradication of such abominable practices as thagi (gross forms of cheating and swindling), ritual murders, slavery, Sati, and clan female infanticide be ignored.[2] But the claim that the British nation is proud of having administered justice to the Oriental people with *impartiality and integrity*[3] is far from true. The partiality displayed in the dispensation of justice in race relations (the Europeans versus the natives), in caste relations (the higher castes versus the lower castes), and in gender relations (the men versus the women) raises serious questions as to the validity of the statement. Nor can it be simply accepted that it never occurred to the colonial rulers that some parts of that justice had been detrimental to the interests of such large groups as peasants and women.[4]

In analyzing women's encounter with colonial criminal justice, this chapter shows how the colonial justice and the penal system were anything but just and full of integrity for women and, how their interests were marginalized in the justice system by the government's decision to legislate and to enforce only some domestic laws. It also deals with women's encounter with the law enforcement agencies; the session judges; and the prison system that victimized and totally depraved them and let them out as an underclass of ostracized women.

The second section of the chapter examines the deportation system of female convicts to the penal colonies and how it affected women.

One important factor in the serious undermining of women's rights in the criminal justice system, as discussed in Chapter 2, was the government's decision to import and to legislate certain English domestic laws, alien to Hindu society. But the unfairness of it was that it required wives, but not husbands, to obey them. Such immunity of husbands from law may actually have encouraged abuse and violence against wives and women generally.

The "Grave and Sudden Provocation" clause in adultery cases, for instance, applied to wives as well as to erring sisters, as the Appellate Criminal case *Queen-Empress vs. Chunni* illustrated.[5]

Chunni, the accused, pleaded in his defense that he had found his sister having an illicit relations with a man and, "in a fit of passion," killed them both on the spot. In deciding his case, the Justices ruled that the crime had been committed "under Grave and Sudden Provocation"; therefore, the crime amounted to culpable homicide and not murder. While noting the difference between the provocation a man received when he found his wife committing adultery and the provocation he received when he found his sister dishonoring his family, the Judges, nonetheless, felt that the "latter provocation could not in common sense and in one's experience of the world, be looked upon as a light one. . . . The law of England was, no doubt, very strict in these matters." Therefore, Chunni was sentenced to five years' rigorous imprisonment for murdering two persons.[6]

With such laws in effect, it is not surprising that a common knowledge had prevailed among the villagers that the *Sarkar* (government) took a merciful view of the killings of wives if the parties were discovered in the very act. And if "sudden provocation" could be established, the offense would then be reduced to one of culpable homicide and not murder.[7]

The case also showed that the English rulers of India did not differ much from Indian patriarchal fathers' notions of definite social roles and sexual behavior of women. Consequently, Indian women became the bearers of the burden of the worst biases of the two cultures. They not only supported each other to punish Hindu women but, where the native culture fell short, English laws stepped in to reinforce them. The colonial rulers also chose to interpret, and to enforce some Hindu laws with more "peremptory distinctiveness" than was to be found in the Hindu code.[8] As oppressive as the Hindu rules had been for women, they were, nonetheless, known to be greatly modified in practice because the observance of the Hindu laws had been lax in the extreme. *The Pioneer* described the laws in the following manner:

> There is reason to believe that those hardships have been aggravated by the application to the Hindu Society of some of the rules of the English law, especially that which enforces "The Restitution of Conjugal Rights," with more peremptory distinctiveness than is to be found in the Hindu code. It would be difficult to find a more curious instance of an archaic institution, preserved by custom to later and more advanced times, and sanctioned and enforced at last, by an alien and unsympathetic code—Nay, the English law-giver has carried oppression still further, for he has imported a process from his own system previously unknown to India, to enforce the rights of a husband against a reluctant wife.[9]

The greatest injustice, however, was done to females when laws needed to protect helpless classes of women—child-brides and widows in particular—were not enacted even when they not only caused much distress but, generated dreadful crimes as well. The fact behind the government's explanation that those issues came under the Hindu "domestic and religious" jurisdictions, and that they, therefore, could not be abolished by legislation, was its rationalization to ignore women's problems and, thereby, avoid offending native patriarchs. Nor was the government's role in native domestic and religious domain so neutral as it repeatedly declared because, as already noted, laws pertaining to domestic affairs had been passed supporting men's interests.

The government's reluctance to interfere in native gender relations affected girls and women grievously. Child-marriages and enforced widowhood continued to affect the health and lives of little girls and women and women's crime pattern; it stood in the way of social reform; it provided men with newer tools to further oppress and victimize women; and most of all, under the cover of "non-interference in domestic and religious affairs of the natives," the rulers left women out of the justice system.

But if some laws disadvantaged women, then the law enforcement agencies—the network of chaukidars and the police—became another instrument of women's oppression and grief. While the chaukidar served a useful purpose as a tool of surveillance for the alien ruling power, they did not, however, help the cause of women at all. Because the much despised chaukidar was rewarded for reporting crimes, he made it his business to know not only of the murders, dacoits, robberies, thefts, but also of the widows in the village, of village sexual intrigues, incests, births and murders of illegitimate infants, and the like. In the pre-colonial period, many offenses involving women may have been merely ignored or hidden. But the coming of the chaukidar as the patrolling and reporting agency in the discovery and punishment of crimes, from the village level to the colonial police system, meant little escape from disgrace and punishment.[10] He regularly played on women's and widows' fears of being disgraced, and frequently accepted bribes and extorted money. The chaukidar was also often the puppet of the village head under whose orders he silenced serious crimes and made false arrests.

Another insult to the injury lay in the coercive methods adopted by police authorities to elicit confessions from the accused.[11] The "third degree" methods, a term of "abuse for any kind of duress and extortion practiced by men in authority upon suspected persons to extract information and admission,"[12] and for extortion of money, were impartially applied to both men and women.

Cases where police stripped women naked to elicit confessions were not rare. In Benares, a head constable and his assistant, after ill-treating a Brahmin and his wife under suspicion of theft, took the woman to the public street, stripped her naked, and abused her to the extent that she had a miscarriage.[13] In Allahabad, an alleged extortion of a confession of guilt by the police was obtained from an innocent widow. She was charged under Section 318 of the Penal Code—for exposure (abandonment) of infants or concealment of birth. The charge was found to be false only when she began serving her three months' prison sentence.[14]

Another typical case of police high-handedness was reported when a woman was convicted for concealing a childbirth. The police had forced her to make a confession of infanticide and, apparently, the medical report they submitted confirmed the childbirth. But before she had been in the jail long, the District Magistrate received a report informing him that the woman was about to give birth. The woman had been threatened by the police to confess or to have a doctor "rip open her stomach to examine her womb." She had not been permitted to talk to anyone for three days until she made the false confession before the court that the baby she was so obviously carrying had already been born.[15] In yet another case, a daughter of one household where a theft had been committed was abused to extort a confession. The police wanted her to confess that she had secretly invited her paramour and it was he who had committed the theft. The ill-treatment and the false accusation of "immorality" caused her to commit suicide by drowning in a well.[16] Another common procedure was flogging; in one case a group of seven *Bhatu* (tribal) women were flogged on "the orthodox surface" by a head constable in Benares to elicit bribes.[17]

Reports of police brutalities are extensive, but suffice it to say that vernacular newspapers as well as the two police inquiries, of 1891[18] and 1912,[19] are replete with accounts of their misconduct. Indecent assault, harassment, confinement and rape of women by the police was often deliberate and based on the police's desire to sexually abuse them; to extort money; and to induce their men folk to withdraw complaints. Molestation of women within the Indian cultural context represented yet another dimension. Because the middle class Indian code of "family honor" (*izzat*) revolved around sanctity and purity of women (as much as it revolved around caste and wealth), the violation of any woman's honor, no matter how trivial in form (for instance, staring at and/or touching women generally, but in particular, in purdah system), not only violated the individual woman herself, but that violation degraded and tarnished the entire family's "*izzat*." It was also in this context, purposely, out of malice, and in retaliation to some enmity, that the police searched zananas (women's quarters);[20] reported theft cases as nothing more than a love affair of some female member of the household who, when caught, accused her paramour of being a thief;[21] and falsely implicated women in adultery.[22]

The reports note that the police themselves committed such grave crimes as theft, dakait, extortion and murder throughout the period of this study.[23] But in spite of all their injustices, crimes, and brutalities, police in many cases were either not punished at all, or were given such light sentences that the issue became another cause for people's dissatisfaction [24] with the law. Therefore, in many instances, to avoid further harassment and extortion, the relatives simply denied molestations of their women by the police.[25]

Again, if the public was fearful of the chaukidars and the police, then they, and women in particular, also had reasons to be discontented with the behavior of some of the Sessions Judges. There were many upright and honorable magistrates and judges who grieved over inflicting injustices upon the poor and sometimes innocent people who were falsely accused of crimes.[26] But there were others (natives and British) who displayed gross high-handedness and partiality in the performance of their duties, particularly in cases dealing with women.

Husbands who battered and/or mutilated their wives were either not punished or were given very light sentences. In one such case, a villager, whose wife had disobeyed him, was fined merely 50 rupees by an Indian judge for hacking her almost to pieces with an ax.[27] In another case, even though an accused confessed of murdering his wife, he was acquitted by the Sessions Judge.[28]

These cases serve to illustrate not only that violent acts were committed against women, but also the difficulty of enforcing laws by the same agencies that accepted the law of a husband over his wife as complete and final. This also partly explains why magistrates disposed of criminal procedures in too summary a manner without asking proper questions, or hearing women's witnesses.[29] As it was, the native women were unaccustomed to appearing in courts, and the justices' impatience, inconsideration, and assumptions of the husband's right over his wife left women outside the justice system.

In rape cases, the same age-old myth that a "woman cannot be raped unless she wants to be raped" was applied generally to ignore rape victims even though that crime was consistently on the rise.[30] Some magistrates believed that, except in cases of young girls, it was rare that a grown woman was ever raped. The only way she could be raped was either when she was drugged or overpowered by several men. And since that was simply not done, they had to be adulterous women who preferred charges when caught.[31]

Such ludicrous statements attributing Herculean strength to females when it suited the male cause need no comments other than pointing out that such ideas had been "coined and propagated by men."[32] In India, every woman knew (and continues to know) that rape meant ostracism and prostitution for the remainder of her life, an existence which in fact was "tantamount to death."[33] Still, such statements as "This crime [rape] has somewhat increased. The percentage of convictions will always continue to be low, as false accusations under this section are so frequent" are to be found in many police reports.[34] And there were occasions when women were counter-charged for reporting rapes under the clause "False Charge," as was the case of *Empress vs. Jamni*. Jamni had complained to the police that she had been raped by one Ram Prasad. She lodged a second complaint with the deputy magistrate. The investigating police, however, reported her case as "false." While Jamni's own petition was pending, she was convicted and imprisoned for six weeks under "False Charge." Later, when Jamni's case was heard, the presiding judge found the first proceeding "irregular."[35]

The major flaw in the criminal justice system was that the colonial government's objective in legislating laws was not so much to safeguard the needs and safety of individual natives as it was to render services and protection to the colonial regime.[36] While the justice system did provide advantages for the high caste/class affluent natives, it at the same time became a means of oppression for women and the poor. But while the alien government was negligent in safeguarding the interests of the poor and the weak, the native chaukidars, police, and some native judges shamefully and blatantly used their power to abuse their own people. And because the colonial power depended upon its network of chaukidars and the police system to preserve peace and order, it was reluctant to punish its abusive officials in a manner that the public deemed just.

Yet, the colonial justice system itself was revolutionary in many ways. Having village crimes reported directly to the police stations helped to remove the jurisdiction of crime control from the village as a whole and to break up the old system. In the former times, social ties deterred crimes, and village Panchayats dealt with crimes and the criminals of the lower classes on a personal basis within the village.[37] The newer system introduced into the villages chaukidars and police, a new social order of men who were insensitive to the villagers' concerns. This impersonalized the village system creating problems nowhere better demonstrated than in the colonial penal system of imprisonment.

The penal system was also markedly different in Hindu and Mughal times from that of the colonial period. Under Hindu Law, punishment of death was applied to a comparatively limited class of cases. The "most severe punishment was not the taking of the life but the taking away of social support"[38] or outcasting. Such punishments as mutilations, confiscation of property, exile for felonies, and fines and floggings for misdemeanor were awarded.[39] With these forms of punishment, the institution of prison system was not necessary, nor was it commonly used under Hindu Law.[40] In Moghul India, punishment took a form of torture; that is, the cutting of the right hand for theft and death by sword for robbery with murder. Such forms of degradation to punish offenders as shaving off the head or riding a donkey with face turned towards its tail with the body covered with dust were also popular.[41] Although imprisonment was prevalent in Muslim India, it was not widely practiced.[42]

Prisons based on the Western model were established by the East India Company in the provinces, but much material is not available on early prison systems.[43] Under imperial rule, however, imprisonment became a tool for social control. Its use touched off a form of a general mania where an enormous number of poor and illiterate agriculturists—men, women, old, and young—who were victims of repeated agricultural distress were all sent to jail indiscriminately even for such minor crimes as the theft of a handful of grains. It was that kind of legal definition of "crime," "criminal," and prescribed "punishment" that basically made the Indian jail population a creation of the colonial government. Further, there was no other system that had a more profound effect on girls and women than the colonial prison system.

In fact, the practice of imprisoning simple village people, including young boys and girls, had a very lamentable outcome. The result of such imprisonment, as of one nine-year-old boy, was described by one Indian Chief Justice in the following terms:

> I complain today, as I did in a similar case yesterday, of the system prevailing in this country by which criminals are manufactured! Yes, manufactured. The chances are that if this boy had been placed in a reformatory or similar school, he would have reformed; but there are no such schools to send these miserable young thieves to; they are thrust into jail and they become hardened criminals before they arrive at manhood.[44]

And the Chief Justice added that if a boy of nine years had been sentenced to whipping and discharged with a warning, the boy would have in all probability been reformed. What the Chief Justice described was the traditional mode of punishment.

The manner of sentencing young boys and girls was no different in the North-Western Provinces and Oudh. The result of labeling every juvenile who had a previous conviction a "habitual," regardless of how "trifling" that first offense was, and sending him/her to the Agra Central Jail, was to turn him/her into a hardened criminal.[45]

The condition of unfortunate little girls was even worse. In spite of Miss Carpenter's[46] devastating report on Indian jails in 1867, over thirty years later, in 1900, it was still being reported that, "It was a deplorable spectacle to witness girls of tender ages ranging from nine to twelve mixing indiscriminately with hardened prostitutes and female criminals of the deepest dye."[47] The imprudent imprisonment of juveniles, more especially of girls, was often the turning point of their lives from which they embarked on a career of prostitution and crime even before they reached womanhood.

In her report, Miss Carpenter noted the dreadful state of the prison discipline. She found it incredible that after a settlement in India of nearly a century and a half, after thousands of British citizens had amassed vast fortunes in the East and had retired happily in England, after the "hard governing authority" of the East India Company was replaced with the "mild rule of Her Most Gracious Majesty and Queen," and after England sent out "so many governors, so many civil servants, and so many missionaries" the "criminals of all classes, old and young, male and female, were in ordinary Indian prisons mixed and mingled together rather like brute beasts than human beings."[48]

She described the prison features as she found them. The prisoners were in irons. One cell in many cases was common to all where crowds were confined and were sleeping together promiscuously. The female wards, where they were separated from men, were superintended and inspected by males only. And there was a general neglect and "a total disregard and absence of industrial schools, reformatories, or educational facilities." Those conditions were common to all the jails she visited both in the Bombay and Madras Presidencies.[49]

And if the case of the male convicts was bad, then, at Ahmedabad, in Guzarat, she found the females generally in a "very low degraded condition and dreadful beyond description. They were confined in gloomy wards attached to small courtyards with only male warders in attendance and the work assigned to them was rough which was distasteful to the male prisoners."[50]

In Bombay, she saw five murderesses locked up together without any attempt to improve them. Upon her suggestion that visits from ladies might benefit them, she was informed that not only was there no place where ladies could sit to instruct the prisoners, but that the "conditions and habits of the women were so filthy that no ladies could approach them."

In Poona, the condition of the women was worse; "forty or fifty women were locked up together, some aged in crime, some murderesses; and some young and interesting looking girls who were here learning crime from their elders."[51] Her entire report was a revelation of the dreadful conditions and miseries experienced by all the prisoners in the colonial jails. What Miss Carpenter did not include in her report, however, was the kind of life that awaited the majority of those girls and women upon their release from the prisons.

And although she did not visit Punjab, the Inspector General of Police, Punjab, reconfirmed her findings as in the other presidencies. His experience of the prisons of the Punjab led the Inspector General of the Police to believe that not only were the "jails not penal and deterrent as they were meant to be, but that the system tended to demoralize the prisoner and return" him/her to the society morally worse than when he/she entered the prison.[52]

It might be noted that the records do not show either Carpenter's visit or her receipt of any report from the jails in the North-Western Provinces and Oudh. One reason may have been that until 1887 all the laws of the Provinces had to be passed by the Viceroy-in-Council.[53] And it is possible that, because any unfavorable report would have been an embarrassment to the Government of India, she either avoided or was not granted permission to visit them. However, the jail conditions of the provinces matched those of the others described by Carpenter.

Following the Jail Committee's recommendation in 1877, some reforms were instituted at the Lucknow Central in the North-Western Provinces and Oudh and other prisons in the country. The female wards were placed outside the jail proper, communication with the male prisoners was eliminated, and a European matron was appointed to be in charge of the women prisoners.[54] The conditions in remote district jails, however, remained perfectly scandalous as late as 1887.

An inquiry in district jails in Madras that year showed that not only were there no female officers in charge, but the cells in which female prisoners were confined were in some cases not even separated from those for the male prisoners.[55] Thus, the inquiry reasonably questioned whether similar conditions did not exist in the jails in the other presidencies as well. It reasoned that the existence of those conditions was really not as rare as they were being stated to be in the annual jail reports. Their *"discoveries were rare"* only because those conditions were *"rarely reported."*[56]

And, indeed, there were reasons to believe that the condition and the treatment of female prisoners in the district jails of the North-Western Provinces and Oudh remained anything but satisfactory even in the closing years of the nineteenth century. In 1895, when the number of female prisoners increased vastly (4,033 against 2,922 in 1894, for instance), the Superintendent of the Jails found an occasion to invite the attention of the authorities to a pertinent extract from a paper read before the Paris Prison Congress of 1895. He found the content of the extract to be relevant to the Indian case as well. Protesting against the corrupting association of women in the prisons, the Congress had observed:

> The common rooms are veritable recruiting offices for the army of debauchery and crime. It is impossible to preserve women from the multiplied enemies who scheme their ruin in prison association; from the thieves, brothel servants, prostitutes, and others around them.[57]

Such fears about women in Indian jails were very real as the proceedings on the need for reformatory schools for young women in 1899 had shown. Their association was with none other than the female warders, the very guardians of the female prisoners of the district jails, who were also the worst possible class of prostitutes and procuresses. They demoralized young girls beyond redemption.[58]

Another weakness in the Indian prison system was a general lack of segregation of the various categories of prisoners. In most cases, females who were still under trial, were kept with the female convicts. That no separate accommodation was provided for them was both morally and legally wrong. Had any unconvicted woman known enough to have taken action against the Inspector-General of Prisons, the law would have held good for damages.[59] It was just as well for the colonial government that almost all the prisoners were poor and illiterate.

The continued lack of night separation of prisoners in Indian jails also remained a serious cause for scandal. In 1893, for instance, an "unnamed high official in India" addressed the problems of the Indian prisons to the Howard Association in England, solely in a private and unofficial capacity, in the following manner:

> I am strongly of opinion that there are certain directions in which the reform of the Indian prison system is greatly called for. I am anxious both that the Howard Association should not be directed to lines on inquiry which would prove erroneous, and that its influence should be brought to bear in those directions where reform is called for. . . . Turning to points immediately connected with prison work, *the crying necessity* of Indian jail administration is the *provision of separate sleeping accommodation* for all classes of prisoners. It needs no demonstration that when 20, 30 or more prisoners are locked up at night in the same dormitory or ward, the more guilty corrupt those who are less experienced in crime. At present *association* sleeping wards are almost the invariable rule in all Indian jails.[60]

The Association followed through the writer's suggestion and urged the Government of India to give a pledge that no more association wards would be built in any province. The Government of India accepted the matter *in principle* to gradually put the proposal in effect as funds permitted. The Government of the North-Western Provinces and Oudh, however, found the idea "utopian" and forwarded the proposal to the Inspector-General of the Jails for *information but hardly for guidance*.[61] What this continued to mean to women, as to all the other classes of prisoners, was that if a female prisoner was not debauched when she entered a jail, then prison conditions soon left her in just such a state.[62]

While the prison conditions were wretched, their release from prisons awaited the female ex-convicts even a more uncertain and a desolate future. It was for that reason that serious apprehensions had been expressed to the Lieutenant-Governor of the provinces as early as 1873. That report stated that when female prisoners were released from jails, they sometimes did not return to their homes, but instead they resorted to immoral lives. Some very sad and "lamentable instances had come to light to substantiate" the report.[63]

The truth, however, was that a very large majority of women ex-prisoners never returned to their homes upon their release from the prisons. Moreover, they did not willingly resort to immoral lives. They were either recruited or forced into it. According to the Hindu custom, when women once left their families and home environments, they became defiled; they were then discarded by their families unless, perhaps, they came from the lowest social rank. This was nowhere better illustrated than in the colonial imprisonment system where ex-convict women were actually being abandoned by their relatives. This was even true of men in certain castes.[64] But, with the British justice system so intent on imprisoning even young girls for such minor offenses as stealing grains when hungry, the number of abandoned ex-women prisoners increased as the following suggests:

> In 1875, it was ascertained that of the 2,162 female convicts released during the year, 993 were living with their *friends*, while 1,169 had neither returned to their homes, nor left any traces of their fate.[65]
>
> In 1876, of 2,120 female convicts released, 954 were received by their *friends* at the jail gates, and 2,194 were left unattended.[66]
>
> In 1877, of 3,768 female prisoners released during the year, 1,574 were received by their *friends* at the jail gates, and 2,194 were left unattended, and their subsequent fate was unknown. But, added the report, probably the greater number of the discharged female prisoners, whose subsequent residence was not traced, were homeless or friendless widows, or deserted wives, who labored in fields or on roads, and had no settled domicile.[67]
>
> In 1878, of 8,157 female convicts released during the year, it had been reported that 3,207 were released to their *friends* at the jail gates, and 4,950 were left unattended.[68]
>
> In 1879, of the 4,492 female prisoners released during the year, 1,482 were made over to their *friends* at the jail gates, and 3,010 were left unattended. It was ascertained that of the whole number, 2,166 returned to

their homes (for 2,166 to have returned home seems a high number because it does not coincide with the figures of the other years) while no information could be obtained regarding the 2,069, other than that 257 of them never returned home.[69]

In 1880, there were 3,488 releases of female prisoners. Notice was sent to the relatives in 2,672 cases, but only *friends* of 1,814 female prisoners received them at the jail gates; fifty-seven were escorted to their homes by female warders, 125 were sent to their homes by rail, and 1,492 were released unattended at the jail gates.[70]

In 1881, of 3,314 females released during the year, 1,721 were made over to their *friends* at the jail gates, 144 were sent to their homes in charge of female warders, 159 were sent by rail to a station near their homes, and 1,290 were released unattended at the jail gates. Information was sent to the relatives of 2,565 females, but the invitation to come and receive their relatives was responded to in only 1,721 cases. Most of the women released at the jail gate were prostitutes, Kanjars, and other homeless wanderers, or old women who lived in the immediate neighbourhood of the jail.[71]

And in 1883, 2,771 women were released; of those 1,513 were made over to their *friends* at the jail gates, 257 were sent away by rail or road in charge of female warders, and 1,001 were released at the jail gate. The latter were mainly prostitutes or gypsies or were women residing in the neighborhood.[72]

The objective of the long review of these judicial criminal statistics of released women prisoners has been to illustrate that, during those eight years, of the 30,372 female prisoners released from prison, 4,629 reached their homes and were accepted by their relatives, and 13,256 found residence with *friends*. The fate of the other 18,341 remained unknown. (There is some discrepancy in the numbers found in the various reports.)

Women who were found to be living not with *relatives* but with *friends* have to be considered as "lost" women also. And for that reason, "friends" has been italicized in the above reviews. The question is, who exactly were those friends who received them at the jail gates? And why was it that they "lived" with friends and not with relatives? And how was it that peasant women from remote areas had friends in places where prisons were located? It is interesting to note that many of those "friends" were none other than the jail officials who themselves recruited many of the female ex-prisoners upon their release outside the prison gates,[73] some perhaps for the army cantonments. The women were most likely enticed away even before they were aware of what was happening. And it would be those same jail officials who recruited female ex-prisoners from outside the jail gates who would enter in the jail records "living with friends." Therefore, 13,256 ex-convicts who were received by *friends* at the jail gates, never arrived at their homes.

For those who were left on the streets, it can be safely concluded that they, too, became victims of brothel keepers, kidnappers, and recruiters. Therefore, what the numbers finally illustrate is that almost all of the female ex-convicts, probably 90 to 95 percent, who entered the prison system never returned to their homes.

The second point to be made is that the jail officials' justification from time to time that a large number of women unaccounted for upon their release from the jails came from among prostitutes, homeless women, old women, gypsies and friendless widows is erroneous. The fact was, and as the jail reports show, that the largest number of female convicts, from 1878 to 1912, was peasant women with families. The next largest number was made up of widows. Unmarried women, mostly juveniles and prostitutes, formed a much smaller percentage, while the total number of old women convicts never reached more than one hundred, except for once.[74] Prostitutes and old women, as shown by the figures in Table 12 above, were the exceptions and not the rule. Therefore, such justifications claiming that the majority of the female ex-prisoners who never arrived home were homeless women, old women, and so on, or that they were being released at the jail gates, far away from their homes with no relatives to meet them, were only marginally true. The fate of the majority of female ex-prisoners was decided by the colonial imprisonment system that put them in jails, their relatives who abandoned them, and by the jail officials and the procurers of prostitutes who recruited them for "immoral" purposes.

That was the real life tragedy of female ex-convicts. Their case is represented by one young woman who was sent home from Partabgarh Jail. Although a female warder had escorted her home, her people refused to have anything to do with her. The young woman was left to go on the streets.[75] In another case, when relatives of a sixteen-year-old girl did not come to receive her at the jail gates, the police, instead of sending her home by rail, walked her a distance of 380 miles. What the sixteen-year-old girl may have suffered at the hands of the police, although not recorded, can well be imagined. The girl, apparently a "habitual," was sent to the Agra Central Jail, not for stealing but for receiving stolen property.[76] Not much can be said of a system that labeled a sixteen-year-old female a "habitual," incarcerated her for *receiving* stolen property, and helped to make her homeless and a prostitute for the rest of her life.

As for prison rules—those that specified the transfer of female prisoners from central prisons to district prisons before their release, so that they could be closer to their homes; that "summoned" relatives to receive ex-prisoners at the jail gates; or that required younger female prisoners to be escorted to their homes—they were not worth the paper they were written on. Since ultimately imprisonment of women meant their abandonment, the jail reports continued to record the largest number of incarcerated women as having "never returned home."

Penal Colonies of the Andaman and the Nicobar Islands and Women Criminals

If the incarceration of women prisoners in the provincial prisons was lamentable, then that of those who were transported to the penal colonies of the Andaman and the Nicobar Islands for serious crimes was deplorable. Their transportation to the penal colonies began only after unnatural vice among the all male convicts in the penal colonies had become evident and the colonial government felt that there was a need for women in the settlement.[77]

The first group of two hundred male convicts (mutineers) had arrived on the Islands on March 10, 1858.[78] And the first group of thirty life-convict females reached the Islands in May of 1860. But the problem with the system was that the number of female convicts who qualified to be transported to the penal colonies always remained too small to fulfill the desired intention of the rulers. For instance, in 1874, there were 7,820 male and 895 female life convicts in the penal colonies.[79] In 1879, of the 2,447 self-supporters, there were only 363 women, a number which amounted to nearly seven men to every woman.[80] And in 1880–1881, the population of 10,851 was made up of 9,757 males and 1,094 females.[81]

Thus, the excessive disproportion of the sexes did not solve any problems. Instead, it only made women prostitutes because they were forced to serve many men and, at the same time, it endangered their lives because sexual jealousies among the men often prompted their murders as well. Reports from the penal colonies substantiate that nearly all the murders and attempts at murder, of both men and women, were directly or indirectly related to the same cause.[82]

This led the government to remove of some of the restrictions against transportation of female term convicts in 1891. Under the original rules, female convicts sentenced for life, and those sentenced for ten years and upwards, were eligible for transportation. Under the revised rules, those serving for terms of seven years and upwards, those who were either unmarried, or widowed, and those who had been divorced or repudiated by their husbands, and were thus free to marry, became eligible for deportation to the penal colonies.[83]

The result of the revised law, however, was not much better. Though the number of females deported rose, from eight in 1891, to twenty-two in

1892, from the provinces,[84] it steadily declined over the years. More than half a century later, in 1913, the Superintendent of Port Blair was still reporting that the number of the convict women in the local jail had declined, and he was still requesting that instructions might be issued for the regular deportation of all life and term female convicts who were eligible under the rules for transportation.[85] Consequently, the state of the morality of the prisoners and the crimes associated with their condition remained unchanged through the years.

The promiscuous nature of the environment in the penal colonies was noted in a report in 1919–1920. It found not a single woman of reputable character in the Western District. The state of the Eastern District was no better.[86] A report in 1890 had given a similar picture.[87] It had described the conditions even more starkly when it gave an account that "a painful amount of prostitution" was also found to exist among the young girls who were born on the Islands. A preponderance of males over females was the cause given for the "wholesale immorality." But the report also justified the existing conditions by noting that convict mothers were "hardly of a class who could bring up their girls to a high morality."[88]

Stereotyping all the convict mothers as such without taking all the factors into account was to seek a justification for the "immoral" policies of the colonial government. While the disproportion of the sexes was the most important factor, the penal settlement was also so designed as to be demeaning and to encourage promiscuity. It was located across the waters and isolated from all the sanctions, restrictions, and reformative influences of a surrounding society. Left to themselves like "brute animals," the convicts allowed their morals to be forgotten.

Moreover, the odd policy of the colonial regime allowing convict marriages was itself looked upon as another source of "incubation of criminality."[89] The offspring of criminal couples, reared in the same atmosphere of crime and promiscuity, also became contaminated.[90] Moreover, when convict mothers could not protect themselves against all the evils and dangers in the penal colonies, how could they then shield their daughters?

But the "immorality" of women had once again become the rallying point of the British Indian Jail Committees as though the colonial government was unaware of the consequences of its own policy of having glaring disproportionate number of male/female convicts transported beginning in 1860. Rather than viewing the system that induced "immorality" as morally wrong, the civilized British rulers explained that "heredity" increased the "immoral character of women" and thereby accounted for a woman's "meaner qualities."[91]

But for the female convicts, their problems did not end with enforced prostitution and debasement of their lives. Many instances from the Annual Administration Reports of the Islands can be quoted to verify that for them murder and threats of murder were also very real. Common motives for such crimes were always directly or indirectly related to sexual jealousies. The following reports give us an idea of the kinds of danger women encountered in the penal colonies:

> On the night of November 21, at Viper Island, convict Kulloo attempted to cut the nose of a female convict named Joomne; having failed the attempt, he attacked her again and attempted to cut her throat with a razor. The motive for his attempt at murder was jealousy.
>
> On June 22, 1876, Govinda Dhobie, a life-convict, murdered his wife, Mussamat Topo, in his house. Cause: jealousy.
>
> In June 1876, Buta Singh, a life convict, murdered female Gujur Bebee in her house with an axe; the cause of murder was jealousy.
>
> On December 15, 1876, Mussamat Zama Bebee was murdered at her house; the crime was not solved.
>
> Case of female Umra Konwar, No. 16154: On March 9, 1879, female Umra Konwar left her hut in the New Clearing. She never returned alive to her house; no proof of criminal harm was found against anyone.
>
> On February 25, 1880, Gunpatipanoo, a self-supporting life convict, attempted to murder the wife of another man, with whom he had an intrigue.
>
> The convict Shafat Khan, while attempting to take the life of a free woman with a kitchen knife, wounded her in the most savage manner. The woman had rejected his improper overtures. The man was sentenced to be hanged.
>
> On August 25, 1881, female Sukhia was found murdered in the Haddo Garden. Her murder remained unsolved.
>
> On August 26, 1894, Mussammat Sobha died of poisoning. One Ramsahai was suspected of the murder but he was not hanged for want of evidence.[92]

The above record presents some examples of another form of gross victimization, hitherto unknown, of the female criminals under the colonial rule.

Nor did married lives bring women, or men, respectability, security, safety, lasting relationships and family lives. With an overwhelming number of convicts without partners, the marriages of the few became another peculiarity of the penal colonies.

Those women who were married, faced yet another problem—desertion by their husbands after their release from the penal settlement.[93] An inquiry in seven districts in the United Provinces showed that the desertion of a woman depended on the caste of the man and the woman. Such marriages, where women differed from the castes of their husbands, were recognized as valid only by the lower caste Hindus. Of those, five couples—sweeper, Kori, Barber and other lower castes—were found to be living together as husbands and wives.[94] But of the higher castes—Brahmans, Thakurs, Chattries, and so on—if the wife was of a lower caste, where according to Hindu law and custom the couple would be looked upon as outcasts by the relatives and the caste-fellows, only one such case was reported. In another case, the man had handed over the woman he had brought from Port Blair to another.

Those seven cases, however, did not provide sufficient evidence to allow one to generalize on the marriages that took place in the penal colonies. But they do show that the lower caste couples formed lasting relationships at times. They also returned to their villages occasionally, perhaps in the knowledge that they would be accepted by their relatives and friends. The higher caste ex-convicts, on the other hand, either did not return or, if they did, then the chances were that they abandoned their lower caste wives.

Finally, the transportation of women convicts was neither a minor punishment nor was it begun in order to give an "advantage" to the women, as it was claimed by the Government of India.[95] The sad truth was that the system itself amounted to no less than state-sponsored prostitution. And though marriages of convicts were permitted, for many women those marriages also became another source of danger and degradation. Therefore, for women who were transported to the penal colonies with the notion of finding marriage and a beginning of a new life, the idea remained just that—an idea. For many naive and simple village women, such as widow Tulsa, who were labeled convicts, numbered, transported and left amid a settlement of depraved convicts, life presented many dangers and uncertainties. In that respect, those who remained in the provincial prisons fared somewhat better.

Ultimately, however, the majority of ex-convict women, whether in the Islands or from the provincial prisons, were forced to embrace prostitution because that was the only place and profession open to them. Nor did the term of incarceration mean much. No matter, whether the sentence of imprisonment was for two to five, or for seven to ten years, women passed through the same system, one which finally left them debauched, deserted, and desolate. The major weakness in the colonial government's penal system was that its focus was on social control through imprisonment. It neither paid any heed to the condition of the prisoners nor made an adequate effort to eradicate or even to mitigate the demeaning conditions that prevailed in the penal system. The result was that the system succeeded only in demoralizing simple village men, women and children and, in making them habitual criminals often for life and often for simple crimes.

If the colonial government's imprisonment policy was meant to be "reformative," or if the avowed object of the transportation system was "a long education to useful citizenship,"[96] then the answer to its success could easily have been found in the conditions of the jails and in the number of female ex-convicts it produced each year as "abandoned" and/or "lost" citizens who were forced to live in hovels outside the social system and practice the lowest forms of prostitution for survival. In the end, the only way the colonial history could firmly establish the morality, the civilizing mission, and the soundness of its own policies was by turning the facts upside down and labeling women "immoral."

NOTES

1. Jaytilak Guha Roy, *Prisons and Society: A Study of the Indian Jail System* (New Delhi: Gian Publishing House, 1989), p. vii.
2. Ibid.
3. J. Duncan M. Derrett, "The Administration of Hindu Law by the British," *Comparative Studies in Society and History*, vol. 1, no. 1 (November 1961): 10.
4. J. Duncan Derrett, p. 10.
5. *ILR.* Allahabad Series, Vol. XVIII. (Allahabad: 1896), p. 1131.
6. Ibid.
7. Cecil Walsh, "False Confession," *Indian Village Crime*, p. 180; and K. L. Gauba, *Famous Trials for Love and Murder* (Lahore: The Lion Press, 1945), pp. 191, 196.
8. James Samuelson, *India, Past and Present*, p. 62. He referred to the 1860 law specifying that marriage of girls may be consummated at age ten; Dorothy Stein in, "Women to Burn: Suttee as a Normative Institution," *Signs* vol. 4, no. 2 (August 1978–September 1979): 264 ; and "The Hindu Woman and the English Public," *Pioneer*, 15 September 1890, p. 15.
9. *Pioneer*, "The Hindu Woman and the English Public," p. 3. The case of widows would be another example.
10. *Report of the Administration of the Police of the United Provinces* for 1902, no. 1922-A/11-14 of 1903, p. 2 ; Cecil Walsh, "The Third Degree," *Crime in India*, p. 280; Miyan Mithu Khan, *Confessions of a Constable* (London: E. J. Lazrus and Co., 1875), pp. 1, 6; and Hollins in *Indian Police Collection*.
11. Ibid.
12. *The Bharat Jivan* (Benares), 4 January, in *Confidential Selections*, 27 December, 1887, p. 211. In this case, the head constable was fined 300 rupees and his assistant was imprisoned for two months.
13. *The Mihir-i-Nimroz* (Bijnor), 22 November, in *Confidential Selections*, 28 November 1881, p. 690.
14. *The Prayag Samachar* (Allahabad), 19 January, in *Confidential Selections*, 20 January 1891, p. 33.

15. *The Halat-i-Hind* (Allahabad), 27 December, in *Confidential Selections*, 6 January 1891, p. 6.
16. *Surma-i-Razgar* (Agra), January, in *Confidential Selections*, 29 January 1891, p. 29.
17. The Evidence of the Police Committee Appointed in 1890 to *Enquire into Certain Questions Connected with the Police Administration of the North-Western Provinces and Oudh* (Allahabad: Pioneer Press, 1891), p. 53. (Hereafter cited as *Police Inquiry of 1890.*)
18. Ibid., p.87.
19. *Police Department Proceedings.* "Enquiries into the Complaints of Police Misconduct," July 1912, File No. 228 of 1911, p. 1. (Hereafter cited as *Police Inquiry of 1912.*)
20. Ibid., p. 75.
21. *Police Inquiry of 1891*, p. 17.
22. *Police Inquiry of 1912*, pp. 14, 16 and 43, 53.
23. *Police Inquiry of 1891*, p. 17; *Police Inquiry of 1912*, pp. 14, 16 and 43, 53; *and North-Western Provinces Justice (Criminal) Administration during the Year 1873*, Extracts, District of Moradabad, pp. 1, 3.
24. *The Nasum-i-Agra* (Agra), 30 September, in *Confidential Selections*, 7 October 1889, p. 691; and *Police Inquiry of 1912*, p. 16.
25. *Police Inquiry of 1891*, p. 48.
26. Cecil Walsh, "False Confession," *Indian Village Crime*, p. 179; and *Pioneer*, 30 June 1890, p. 2.
27. Cecil Walsh, *Indian Village Crime*, p. 35.
28. *Pioneer*, 2 October 1890, p. 2.
29. *Weekly Notes of the Cases Decided by the High Court*, May 30, Criminal Reference Rukmin v. Peare Lal Husband and Wife—Maintenance of Wife—"Cruelty"— (Allahabad: 10 August 1889).
30. *Police Reports for 1881*, no. 1552A of 1882, p. 2: and no. 352-VI-136-1915 of 1915, p. 6.
31. *Police Reports for 1879*, no. 851A of 1880, p. 2; for 1880, no. 1250 of 1881, p. 1; and for 1881, no. 1522A of 1882, p. 18.
32. Ram Ahuja, *Crime Against Women*, p. 6.
33. Ibid., p. 6.
34. *Police Reports for 1879*, no. 851A of 1880, p. 2; for 1880, no. 1250 of 1881, p. 1; and for 1881, no. 1522A of 1882, pp. 1–2.
35. *ILR.* Allahabad Series, Vol. V, 1883, Empress v. Jamni, False Charge—Act XLV of 1860 (Penal Code), 9 March 1883, pp. 370–372.
36. David Arnold, "Crime and Crime Control in Madras, 1858–1947," in *Crime and Criminality in British India*, p. 77.
37. David Mandelbaum, *Society in India: Continuity and Change*, p. 305; and H. R. Fink, "Crimes and Punishment under Hindu Law," p. 31.
38. Jaytilak Guha Roy, *Prisons and Society*, pp. 5, 9.
39. Sushil Chandra, *Sociology of Deviation in India* (Bombay, New York: Allied Publishers, 1967), pp. 197, 198.
40. H. R. Fink, "Crimes and Punishments under Hindu Law," p. 130; and Sushil Chandra, *Sociology in Deviation*, pp. 197, 98; and Jaytilak Guha Roy, *Prisons and Society: A Study of the Jail System*, p. 5.
41. Jaytilak Guha Roy, *Prisons and Society*, p. 5; and H. R. Fink, "Crimes and Punishments under Hindu Law," p. 130.
42. Ibid.

43. Sushil Chandra, *Sociology of Deviation in India*, pp. 197, 98.
44. Diwan Bahadur R. Ragonatha Rao, "Punishment by Imprisonment," *Pioneer*, 10 May 1890, p. 2.
45. Ibid. It was not until October 1899 that a Depot for Girl Convicts, which was attached to the Female Central Jail in Lucknow, was opened under the supervision of an especially appointed matron. Habitual girls were kept entirely separate from them. And all the girls upon release were accompanied to their native districts by a matron. *Jail Reports for 1899*, no. 3700/H-45 of 1900, p. 5.
46. Miss Carpenter, "Our Mission Work in India." The article was printed in the *Edinburgh Courant*, 15 October 1887. It was included in the *Report Jails and Jail Discipline in India 1867–1868*, by A. P. Howell, Under Secretary to the Government of India: With Extracts from the Jail Reports of the several Governments and Administrators under the Government of India for the Year 1867. Calcutta, 1868. Office of Superintendent of Government. Part 1, Appendix, p. 69. (Hereafter cited as *Carpenter's Report*.)
47. *Jail Reports for 1900*, no. 3200/H-48 of 1901, p. 4.
48. *Carpenter's Report*, p. 69.
49. Ibid.
50. Ibid., p. 70.
51. Ibid., p. 71.
52. Ibid.
53. Dharma Bhanu, *History and Administration of the North-Western Provinces*, p. 2. It was not until 1888 that the North-Western Provinces and Oudh were given a Legislative Council to help the Lieutenant-Governor in his legislative work. Dharma Bhanu, ibid., p. 2.
54. *The Judicial (Criminal) Department Proceedings, North-Western Provinces and Oudh*, "Entertainment of Matrons and Female Warders on the Prison Staff in which Female Prisoners Are Confined." February 1888, File No. 62B, p. 2. This inquiry came about as a result of a memorandum by Sir E. DuCane, on Prisons in India, dated 17 September 1887. Ibid.

The Prison Act of 1865 required a matron and necessary female officers at every prison in which women were confined. And the Prison Act of 1877 specified that no male officer or visitor be allowed to enter the female division of the prison except when accompanied by a female officer. However, according to the reports, those provisions were often violated.

Although the Prisons Acts of 1894 made some progress, it was not until 1919 when Indian Jail Committee took a modern and progressive approach to prison reformation. Ahmed Siddique, *Criminology: Problems and Perspectives* (Lucknow: Eastern Book Company, 1983), p. 101.
55. Ibid.
56. Ibid.; emphasis added.
57. *Jail Reports for 1895*, no. 5311A of 1896, p. 2. The paper was written by Madame D'Abbadir D'Arrast, Secretary of the Paris "Patronage" Society, in the *Jail Reports for 1895*.
58. *The Judicial (Criminal) Department Proceedings*, "Reformatory School for Female Criminals," April 1899, File No. 768C, p. 39.
59. *Jail Reports for 1897*, no. 3897/H-18 of 1898, p. 3. These remarks were made by Mr. Rose, the Commissioner of Agra Division, which the Superintendent of the Jails found to be true in his inspection of the jails. Ibid., p. 3.
60. *Judicial (Criminal) Department Proceedings*, "Confinement of Prisoners Separately by Night," June 1894, File No. 378C, pp. 174, 177.

61. Ibid., p. 174; emphasis added.
62. *Jail Reports for 1896*, no. 4103/H-48 of 1897, p. 2.
63. *Judicial (Criminal) Department Proceedings*, Resolution No. 537A, 3 April 1873, in Proceedings for February 1888, File No. 62B, p. 5. The proportion of the two denominations, Hindu and Muslim, in the jails was pretty steady; up to 1877, 84 or 85 percent were Hindus and 14 or 15 percent were Muslims, figures which closely represented the proportion of the free population. But from 1879, the Muslim number increased to 20.1 percent and that of the Hindus declined to 79.6 percent. *Jail Reports for 1879*, no. 42 for 1880, p. 3. And it appears the ratio remained unchanged through the period of this study.
64. William Crooke, "The Effect of Imprisonment on Caste," *Notes and Queries*, October 1895, p. 116.
65. *Jail Reports for 1876*, no. 45 of 1877, p. 8.
66. *Jail Reports for 1877*, no. 71 of 1878, p. 14.
67. *Jail Reports for 1878*, no. 74 for 1879, p. 14.
68. *Jail Reports for 1879*, no. 42 of 1880, p. 40.
69. *Jail Reports for 1880*, no. 75 of 1881, p. 7.
70. *Jail Reports for 1881*, no. 50 of 1882, p. 9.
71. *Jail Reports for 1883*, no. 217 of 1884, p. 1.
72. *Jail Reports for 1884*.
73. *Report on the Administration of the North-Western Provinces*, 1875-76 (Allahabad: North-Western Provinces Government Press), 1877, p. 57; and *Judicial (Criminal) Department Proceedings*, "Reformatory School for Female Criminals," April, 1899, File No. 768C, p. 44.
74. *Jail Reports, Statement 11—Judicial (for Convicts Only) Showing the Religion, Age, Previous Occupation of the Convicts Admitted into the Jails of the North-Western Provinces and Oudh*, for the given years.
75. *The Judicial (Criminal) Department Proceedings*, "Escort of Female Prisoners to Their Homes on Release from Jail," January 1886, File No. 342, p. 1; and *Jail Reports for 1886*, no. 2084 of 1887, p. 2.
76. *The Judicial (Criminal) Department Proceedings*, "Escort of Female Prisoners to Their Homes on Release from Jail," January 1886, File No. 342, p. 1.
77. From the Inspector-General of Prisons to the Superintendent of Jails, North-Western Provinces, Circular No. 97 of 1875, Allahabad, 17 July 1875, p. 8; and Iqbal N. Singh, *The Andaman Story* (New Delhi: Vikas Publishing House Private Ltd., 1978), pp. 47, 49 and 180, 190. The Andamans and Nicobar Islands (Indian Territory), a group of more than 300 islands, cover an area of 8,249 kilometers and are situated in the Bay of Bengal. They are approximately 780 miles from Calcutta and 740 miles from Madras, both by sea. A requirement for a harbor in the Andamans by Britain had brought about the idea of founding a penal settlement in the islands in 1856. But while the matter was being deliberated, the Mutiny of 1857 broke out and the need to imprison mutineers led Great Britain to annex the islands on January 22, 1858.

The deplorable conditions in the penal colonies did not become known until journalists and political prisoners began to be transported beginning early in the twentieth century (Iqbal N. Singh, *The Andaman Story*, pp. 47, 49 and 180, 190). It was there that Lord Mayo, the Viceroy and Governor-General of India, was assassinated while visiting the penal colonies on February 8, 1872 by a convict, Sher Ali, ibid., p. 108.
78. I. N. Singh, *The Andaman Story*, pp. 47, 73.

79. L. P. Mathur, *History of the Andaman and Nicobar Islands, 1856–1966* (New Delhi: 1986), p. 165; and I. N. Singh, *The Andaman Story*, p. 113.
80. L. P. Mathur, *History of the Andaman and Nicobar Islands*, p. 169.
81. *Jail Reports for 1892*, no 2992/H-48 of 1893, p. 3.
82. *Annual Report (Home) Department on the Settlement of Port Blair and the Nicobars*, for various years; and L. P. Mathur, p. 165.
83. *Jail Reports for 1892*, no. 292/H-48 of 1893, p. 3.
84. Ibid., p. 3.
85. *Abstract of Correspondence, Judicial (Criminal) Department*, "Transportation of Convicts—Deportation of Female Convicts Both Life and Term to the Andamans," File No. 488/1913, p. 2.
86. *Report of the Indian Jail Committee 1919–1920*, Chp. XXI, para 548, p. 276, quoted in L. P. Mathur, *History of the Andamans and Nicobar Islands*, p. 165.
87. Ibid., p. 173.
88. Ibid.; and H. L. Adams, *Oriental Crime* (London: T. Werner Laurie, 1908), p. 346.
89. *Report of the Annual Settlement (Home) Department, Port Blair and the Nicobars for 1874–75*, No. 443, p. 118.
90. H. L. Adams, *Oriental Crime*, p. 346.
91. Ibid.
92. *The Moral and Material Progress of India, for 1861–1862, Port Blair*. Chapter VII, pp. 187–191, and other Administration Reports.
93. *Judicial (Criminal) Department Proceedings of the Government of the United Provinces*, "The Question of the Extent to Which Convict Marriages in the Andamans Are Recognized in India after the Release of the Parties," File No. 410 of 1914, p. 1.
94. Ibid.
95. *Proceedings of the Police Department for 1890*, File no. 219A, p.117; and "Rules Regarding the Submission to Government of the Cases of Women Murdering Their Children," File no. 142.
96. *The Proceedings of the Government of India*, File No. 142, p. 5; L. P. Mathur, *History of the Andamans and Nicobar Islands*, p. 63; and I. N. Singh, *The Andaman Story*, p. 120.

5

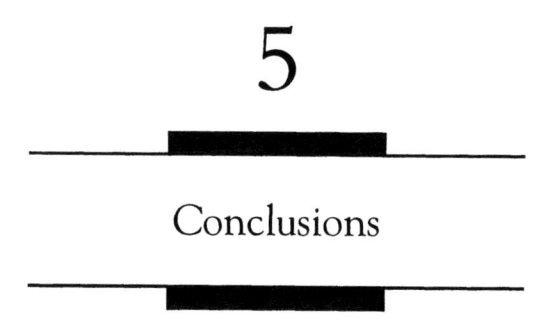

Conclusions

In this study, political economic theory has been used in its broadest sense, one incorporating in its framework the victimization, criminalization, and punishment of women in the North-Western Provinces and Oudh (changed to the United Provinces of Agra and Oudh in 1901) in colonial India. By using the concept of colonial state formation as an ongoing process,[1] it has been presented here that the colonial state hegemony was not merely confined to capitalist economic expansion. Its impact was felt in all spheres: economic, political, domestic, religious, civilian, and in criminal justice and penal systems. Thus, women's oppression and victimization was not limited to economic development alone but permeated every structure of the colonial domination.

I have shown that under colonialism a large majority of women's crimes originated from their victimization, therefore, there was always an ambiguity between their being victims and/or criminals. Centering the study around these victim and criminal females, I have contended that indeed, there were profound changes for women under colonial rule. But those changes were not for the better for a large majority of the women. And, in fact, the "colonial culture" that degraded and exploited women for over a century, though it has been reformulated, has continued to make its impact felt in the post-independence period.

The victimization and criminalization of women in the colonial setting dealt with here formed a complex process. Various ideologies and "divide and rule" policies to divide men from women along gender lines, to divide men from men, and women from women on caste and class lines, were adopted to serve and to safeguard colonial rule. At the same time, the policies leading to women's victimization were often directly or indirectly related to the political motivations of the state in its formation.

The inherent inferior position of women, their subjugation and oppression, was, however, not totally new to the Hindu system. The demeaning terms used to describe the character and conduct of women in Hindu law books, myths, and legends[2] is remarkable. The widow has been especially denounced, her penitential hardships rigorously prescribed, and her social humiliation emphasized in every possible manner.[3]

Moreover, one group of oppressors was represented by women themselves—the Hindu mothers-in-law.[4] Another group of women that was no less capable of ruthless brutality and cold-blooded murder was the women zamindars.[5] They were as capable of placing unreasonable demands and of inflicting injustices upon their tenants as were any male zamindars.[6] Describing them as a class, and in particular those who had partly broken through the *purdah* (the veil system), Walsh noted:

> She [was] often steeped in religious bigotry and in a narrow-minded vindictiveness towards her neighbour or an erring servant. She broke the purdah whenever it suited her, although she preserved the appearance of it, partly from habit and partly from a feminine appreciation of its value as a weapon both of defense and attack.[7]

But it was the colonial restructuring of the economy and the rural society that introduced newer kinds of exploitation and oppression of the lower castes and classes of women in particular, leading them to commit many crimes. This process has been analyzed in Chapter 1, where it has been shown that it was peasant exploitation and indebtedness far more than failure of rains and crops that caused hunger and starvation. The fact that peasants lived a semi-starved existence even in the absence of scarcities and famines shows that recurring scarcities and famines were partly man-made.

After losing its traditional form of employment, the landless class of peasant women lost its subsistence as well and formed an "indefinite and unproductive" class. Many found it difficult to earn daily sustenance for their children and themselves even under normal circumstances. They resorted to petty thefts, prostitution, begging, and the like. The result was an increase in the female crime rate with a corresponding large number of female prisoners in the jail population.

Another factor to worsen women's economic condition under the colonial rule was the absence of their husbands. Many men left or deserted their families during the difficult periods of scarcities and famines, and many left because of the government's labor emigration policy. Women were left alone to care for and to feed hungry children. I have illustrated how crimes of murder of children and murder-suicides by many mothers were directly related to the economic transformation that gave rise to scarcities, poverty, and abandonment of wives by their husbands. One such case showed that a woman in Sitapur killed her infant child by holding it under water until it was dead. That woman had no means of subsistence, and she could not support the child.[8] In another such case, a woman in Mirzapur, unable to support herself and her infant because of poverty, jumped into the River Ganges with the child in her arms. The child drowned, but she was taken out alive.[9]

The criminal records also show that such women's crimes as adultery, prostitution, poisoning, kidnapping, and the murder of children for the jewelry they were wearing increased each year. Those crimes were long-term consequences of women's general economic depression.

One woman poisoner, for example, who called herself Gendao, managed to poison the food of some travelers to Cawnpore. When they became insensible, she escaped with their property. As Jairaji, she drugged an old shopkeeper. It turned out that her real name was Sheoraji, and she had already been convicted and sentenced to seven years' rigorous imprisonment for an earlier similar offense. The woman had become a professional poisoner.[10] Such cases of women poisoners, kidnappers, and murderesses who roamed the provinces come as a surprise because, as Maria Mies has observed recently, "women are still so handicapped with patriarchal norms and institutions that they dare not move beyond the radius of the cities and towns."[11] This statement appears to have been even more true of most nineteenth-century women. Economic changes, poverty, and changes in the traditional family structure may explain why women roamed around committing crimes.

If the restructuring of the economy introduced newer kinds of peasant exploitation, then in Chapter 2 I showed how the collusion between the British colonial rulers and native patriarchs in the interests of security and stability of the colonial rule after the Mutiny may have increased domestic violence. It was not only the literal interpretation and adaptation of Hindu laws which were applied flexibly under Hindu custom, but also the application of some English laws to the Hindu society and requiring women alone to obey them that encouraged abuse. The result was that an increasing number of wives found recourse in suicide and murdered their children in the process.

Another group of women caught in colonial-patriarchal politics was widows. It is not strange that to institute reforms affecting them, the government should have sought the approval of that same hypocritical section of native society whose interests it protected. The extent to which the native patriarchy itself was willing to sink was represented by the Brahmans. For example, in one case, some Brahmans had accepted a caste-fellow's illicit relationship with a widow of the carpenter class for years. But when they ostracized the "sinner," it was not for his "immoral" living, but for his having eaten a *luddoo* (sweet cake) prepared by the widow.[12] That occurrence was by no means a solitary one. It was reported that the public opinion in India was "consistently silent" about such matters.[13]

The colonial government also, by its unwillingness to institute needed reforms for women that would not meet with the approval of the native patriarchy, indirectly became a party to both the creation of a large number of widows and to such crimes as abortion, illegitimate infanticide, and prostitution that resulted from enforced widowhood. Although the role of the government in gender relations pertaining to domestic and religious matters was not totally neutral, it found in the policy of "non-interference in religious and domestic matters of the natives" just that needed rationalization to forestall reforms sorely needed to help young girls and women.

Moreover, by showing little hesitation in punishing widows for their crimes—the very crimes it refused to prevent through legislation—the government agreed with the Hindu society that widows, many of whom were forced to be widows in the first place, were alone both morally and legally guilty.

Such interpretations that construe illegitimate births and infanticide as solely women's problems continue to persist, as the following statement shows: "Though it is hardly a crime in the same sense, one form of killing (or, at least, an offense that presumed that violence had been done) was much more exclusive to women—infanticide."[14] Infanticide was no laughing matter, either to the infant or to the mother in any society. Furthermore, one does not search far for the reason why infanticide "was much more exclusive to women."

In colonial India, illegitimate infanticide was a heinous crime. Women paid a heavy price for the offense in the form of capital punishment, transportation for life to the penal colonies, and imprisonments for varied terms. But why only widows were given severe punishments for infanticide is not clear. There appear to have been very few convictions of the clan-members (Rajputs in particular) who practiced female-infanticide. There is no evidence in the records to indicate that they were ever transported or executed for the same crime. The Female Infanticide Act of 1870 was also not punitive. (Only small fines were imposed on those who broke the law.)[15] It was reformative only in that the clans were encouraged to eliminate dowry practices, the major cause of female infanticide.[16] But legally, infanticide was infanticide, no matter if it was committed because of a family's desire to avoid an expensive dowry, or because of a widow's fear of condemnation. The only conclusion to be drawn from this comparison is, again, policy was a matter only of the power-politics of the colonial rulers. It also leads one to the conclusion that it was a question of legitimacy versus illegitimacy as well. Moralization and modernization of the society was a part of the colonial policy; therefore, in this case, the punishment was based on both moral and legal questions.

While domestic/religious related violence and oppression of women and women's consequent crimes afflicted both the upper and the lower castes and classes of women, the victimization of women in civilian life was solely confined to the lower caste/class women. It has been illustrated in Chapter 3 that no other class suffered the same degree of use, abuse, dishonor, and victimization under the colonial rule as did the lowest caste/class of women. Their morality and their very personal rights were usurped by the magistrates in the courts under the orders of the state itself. The colonial ideology that the lower castes/classes of women had no morals to violate was actually used to demoralize them and then to procure them for prostitution in the army cantonments.

Another line the officials were fond of quoting to explain most unsolved village intrigues and murders was taken from a Persian proverb, "Gold, Land, and Women."[17] Women were perceived as sexual objects, and their relative scarcity made them valuable commodities, as Leacock has pointed out.[18] This was perhaps nowhere better illustrated than in Northern India. The Persian proverb provided the rulers with yet another justification to explain unsolved murders as "intrigues" and "sexual jealousies," as eventualities linked with native women's immoral character. That the village murders may have originated from below, from the men of the lower castes and classes in retaliation to the abuses of their women by the higher castes and classes of men, did not enter the picture even when numerous police cases supported such findings.[19]

I have contended that the unsupervised system of emigration became another factor in kidnapping,[20] forceful confinement, violence, and sexual harassment of the lower-class women. I have also discussed how the colonial government in its monopolization of the cultivation, manufacture, and sale of alcoholic drinks for the excise duty it garnered added another dimension of grief and degradation to the lives of women. The new method of paying in advance for the manufacture of alcoholic drinks, the opening of shops in many villages for the sale of alcohol, and the credit system allowing native men to purchase intoxicants easily helped to spread the consumption of liquor widely. Its ensuing effect on the poor, as was evidenced by the Temperance Society, only led to more poverty, more crime, and more violence against many wives—and to many unhappy homes.

The meeting of the two cultures had a profound impact on social and economic values. The weakening of the family structure resulted in increased violence against women. The murders of "unknown" women were frequently reported in the papers; for example, the case of an unidentified body of a young woman was found in a lake in Allahabad.[21] Another body, naked, was discovered in a well near the Government Press at Allahabad. But what is more revealing is the report that *such cases were rather too frequent at Allahabad.*[22]

In the foregoing chapters, I have analyzed how the focus of the colonial state on the imprisoning of the masses, rather than on the improving of their economic conditions, meant that both widespread poverty and an increasing jail population were creations of the colonial rule. The priority given to social control was seen in the 1935–1936 budget, here to underscore the continuation of these practices after 1910, when the British Indian Government allocated 203 million rupees for the administration of justice, jails, and police, 27 million rupees for agriculture, and 9 million rupees for industry.[23] That tremendously distorted allocation between the economic needs of the people and social control was not an unusual policy of the colonial rule.

Continuing that analysis, it has been shown that the colonial justice system for most women when they faced the law was anything but "just." While the network of native chaukidars and police served the colonial need of detecting and reporting crimes, they regularly raped women, applied brutal and coercive methods to elicit confessions, as well as bribing innocent villagers. The magistrates, for their part, Europeans and natives alike, often violated the rights of women.[24] For instance, one may justly ask what right a deputy magistrate (British in this case) had in dragging an innocent widow on an anonymous accusation and having her examined by a doctor to verify that she was not pregnant.[25] It would seem the colonial government had assumed dictatorial powers to oversee women's "morality." It is no wonder, then, that the magistrates were occasionally assaulted and murdered by peasants.[26]

But however deplorable was the government's practice of procuring innocent women for prostitution through its court system, deplorable, too, was the colonial prison system. I have shown how the prison system only succeeded in manufacturing deviants and how it thoroughly demoralized and debauched the female prisoners. Many simple and naive peasant women and girls (and men and boys) who were not criminals in the real sense of the term were put into the prisons only to be let out as ex-convicts beyond redemption. Again, no matter how demeaning their lives were in the provincial prisons, the experiences of the women convicts in the penal colonies of the Andaman and the Nicobar Islands have to be the most lamentable records in the formation of the colonial capitalist state.

Yet another sad feature of imprisoning women and girls indiscriminately for petty thefts and the like was that those female ex-prisoners could never return to their homes. Most joined the world of an underclass of women who subsisted by begging and by the lowest types of prostitution. It was this class of thousands of "fallen women," reported to be "literally alone in the world," who went to hospitals to die. They were poor, friendless, and had led "sinful lives."[27] It was reported that no native woman would have gone to a hospital if she had a home or anyone to care for her.[28]

It has been contended in the foregoing chapters that the colonial state formation was a continuing process which utterly restructured the economic and social lives of the rural society. The total impact of the unforeseen as well as the deliberate policies of the colonial rule had a sad impact on women. Their victimization and criminalization became part and parcel of that same changing process. The rhetoric of calling and labeling a large majority of women "immoral" was also a colonial invention to exploit the helpless class of females.

There is, on the other hand, no doubt that the ultimate forms of crimes against women practiced by some Hindus in some regions of the country that sorely needed to be abolished were outlawed. Nor could the genuine concerns of many of the officials who witnessed and lamented the gross injustices, the horrible poverty, starvation, disease, and death of the masses be underestimated. But there was little they could do, for the policies to improve the conditions of the people lay in the hands of the Provincial Government and the Government of India. The extent of the Supreme Government's intervention in matters of reform for women, however, remained confined to collecting evidence of their crimes throughout the country and to having them punished by the local authorities.

Finally, while colonial histories have emphasized and re-emphasized the abolition of Sati and female infanticide as examples of civilizing missions of colonial rule, they have remained silent on the justice system's failure to protect child-brides and widows. The victimization and criminalization of an unknown number of twenty-six million widows was a continuing problem, on a much wider scale than was Sati, under colonialism.

The history of the female ex-convicts and of how the colonial prison system produced an underclass of approximately 25,000 ostracized women in eight years—in the North-Western Provinces and Oudh alone—and women who could never again become a part of their families and societies has not been written. Nor have the colonial government's deliberate policy in creating shameful living conditions of the female convicts and their victimization in the penal colonies been mentioned. The role of the government itself, that illegally used its own legal system to demoralize and to procure women for the cantonments, has not been made known. The starving mother-murderesses, the emigration system, the penal system, the story of the penal colonies, the widows, the concubinage system, and the underclass of ostracized women were all surely a part of that same colonial history as were the abolition of Sati and clan female infanticide.

In studying the lives of women below the level of high caste/class, one has to re-evaluate the meaning of the claim that the impact of the colonial progressive influences on women was profound.[29] Looked at from below and in a longer time frame, this claim is hollow. The oppression of women in North India and, generally in India, continues even today and still is explained as it always was in terms of its "culture against females."[30] Such concepts of culture only lead to static explanations of history. They suggest that, because the oppression of women has been a part of the culture, therefore women's conditions have remained unchanged and will remain so. Whereas colonial history shows us that, for better or for worse, changes occur continually. Correlatively, such interpretations also dissociated colonial history from the post-colonial period when India became "modern." While Hindu women's inferior position in society has been an acknowledged fact, the generally negative impact of the "colonial culture" on women was so profound and so prolonged that to expect their exploitation to suddenly disappear with independence would be truly unrealistic.

As it happened, independence brought no social revolution to change the structure of the society, or the "culture of colonialism." While laws have been enacted to give women equal rights and to better their lives, changes for them under a new patriarchal society have been slow in coming because failure to enforce those laws continues. And, just as police brutalities have continued,[31] and just as independence has not been able to overcome the deep social divisions created by colonialism—such as caste relations, religious differences, and the elite/mass dichotomy—so, too, the oppression of women has not been overcome.

In fact, what Maria Mies has concluded in today's context—that "the most brutal forms of violence and of sexist terror" in India are to be found in areas of capitalist development[31]—began long ago under the colonial rule. Therefore, the question of women in India's developmental process since independence is very much "related to the colonial question."[33] Their oppression and victimization cannot be merely attributed to the "culture" of an ancient era.

Moreover, the lower castes/classes of people who suffer atrocities today[34] under the new nation state are the offspring of the same classes who were made landless and homeless by the thousands, who died in tens of thousands of starvation and pestilence, and who were transported by the thousands to develop imperial colonies abroad during the colonial period. Their women were prostituted, victimized, and criminalized. Social violence, therefore, cannot be simply explained in terms of culture, as Ranjana Kumari has appropriately argued; rather, they must be located "in the . . . environment of social change and its accompanying tension."[35]

Finally, the hope for village women to overcome their oppression is in their own organization, as was observed in the Simon Report some sixty years ago: "The women's movement in India holds the key of progress, and the results it may achieve are incalculably great."[36] In recent years, peasant women have begun to organize their own movement against patriarchal-capitalist exploitation, violence, and sexual abuse.[37] That is their best hope.

NOTES

1. C. W. Gailey, *Kinship to Kingship: Gender Hierarchy and State Formation in the Tongan Islands*, p. ix.
2. Professor Wilson, "Hindu Tales," quoted in *Papers on India Reform*, p. 8.
3. Pandita Ramabai, *The High Caste Hindu Women* (Philadelphia: 1888), p. 65.
4. S. C. Dutt, *The Works of Shoshee Chunder Dutt*, p. 222; William Monier, "Zenana Missions," *Papers on Indian Reform*, p. 17; and S. S. Dua, *Society and Culture in Northern India, 1850–1900*, p. 27.
5. Cecil Walsh, "The Fate of the Watchdog," *Indian Village Crimes*, p. 64; and Kapil Kumar, *Peasants in Revolt*, pp. 29, 30.
6. Ibid.
7. Cecil Walsh, "The Fate of the Watchdog," p. 84.
8. *Police Reports for 1888*, no. 1715A of 1889, p. 10.
9. *Police Reports for 1891*, no. 1521A of 1891, p. 6.
10. North-Western Provinces and Oudh (Police) Department, *Annual Report on Special Crime for 1890*, July 1891, File no. 5272A, p. 231.
11. Maria Mies, *The Lace Makers of Narsapur*, p. xi.
12. Mr. Malabari, "The Letter and the Spirit," quoted in *The Statesman*, July 31, 1888, p. 4.
13. Ibid.
14. J. M. Beattie, "The Criminality of Women in Eighteenth-Century England," *Journal of Social History*, 8.4 (1975): 80–118. Judges and juries in Surrey went out of their way to acquit women charged with the crime of infanticide (ibid., p. 84; and R. W. Malcolmson, "Infanticide in the Eighteenth Century," *Crime in England, 1550–1800*, ed. J. S. Cockburn [Princeton: Princeton University Press, 1977], p. 191). But such was not the case in India.
15. *The Moral and Material Progress for the Year 1871–72*, p. 108.
16. Ibid.
17. William Crooke, *The North Western Provinces of India*, p. 142; and Cecil Walsh, *Indian Village Crime*, p. 22.
18. Mona Etienne and Eleanor Leacock, eds., *Women and Colonization: Anthropological Perspectives* (New York: Praeger Publishers, 1980), pp. 17–22.
19. Cecil Walsh, "A Study in Compromise," *Indian Village Crime*, p. 137; *Police Reports for 1902*, no. 1922A of 1903, p. 7; and *Police Report for 1913*, no. 349-VI-159-1914 of 1914, p. 2. The murdered men were all zamindars who had dishonored women of the villages.
20. For instance, the 1875 *Police Report* noted that "after infanticide the subject of kidnapping was most important." *Police Reports for 1874*, no. 820A of 1875, p. 37. Almost forty years later, it was still being reported that "kidnapping is very prevalent and shows a tendency to increase." The reason given was the large

demand for women in Punjab and Sind, the newly formed canal colonies. *Police Report for 1912*, no. 359/VI-167/1913 of 1913, p. 8.
21. *The Prayag Samachar* (Allahabad), 13 December, in *Confidential Selections*, December 1894, p. 221.
22. Ibid., 19 March 1896.
23. L. S. Stavrianos, *Global Rift: The Third World Comes of Age* (New York: William Morrow and Company, Inc., 1981), p. 528.
24. Vernacular papers also continually complained of the brutal and loose conduct of Europeans and the lack of punishment given them, for example, a report in *The Dhela Akhbar* (Moradabad), 8 April, in *Confidential Selections*, 18 April 1896, p. 189.
25. *The Rajputana Gazette* (Ajmere) 8 June, in *Confidential Selections*, 14 June 1888, p. 403.
26. A Late Indian Editor (anon.), *The Murder of Indian Judges: Showing the Causes for Disaffection in India* (London: Simpkin and Marshall, 1871), p. 110. According to this English author, two judges were murdered in 1871. One was a British judge in Calcutta, and the other, a native judge in Lahore. A third, a British official in Lahore, was a victim of an attempted murder (p. 110). The author contends that not one covenanted British Civil Officer, whom he had known for their shocking malpractices, was ever criminally charged by the colonial government. They were all simply allowed to retire with full benefits.
27. Miss Leslie, *Woman's Work in the Indian Mission Field*, Calcutta Decennial Missionary Conference reprint (Calcutta: Baptist Mission Press, 1883), pp. 26, 28.
28. Ibid.
29. Mrs. H. Gray, "The Progress of Women," *Modern India and the West*, pp. 445, 483.
30. Barbara D. Miller, *The Engendered Sex: Neglect of Female Children in Rural North India* (Ithaca: Cornell University Press, 1981), p. 15. Millers's concern has been female infanticide. Although North India has had a recorded history of female infanticide, the practice is not confined to North India.
31. For example, see Baxi's commentary on police brutality in the post-independence period: Upendra Baxi, *Alternatives in Development: Law, the Crisis of the Indian Legal System* (New Delhi: Vikas Publishing House Pvt. Ltd., 1982). The police continue to be responsible for a large number of rapes each year. See Ahuja Ram, *Crime Against Women*, p. 6; and Maria Mies, "Class Struggles and Women's Struggles in Rural India," in *Women: The Last Colony*, pp. 136, 137.
32. Maria Mies, *Women: The Last Colony*, p. 127.
33. Ibid.
34. Ibid., p. 137.
35. Ranjana Kumari, "Dowry Victims: Harassment and Torture," in *Widows Abandoned and Destitute Women in India*, eds. Pramila Dandvate, Ranjana Kumari, and Jamila Verghese (New Delhi: Radiant Publishers, 1989), p. 23.
36. *Report of the Indian Statutory Commission* (Simon Report), vol. 1 (London: HMSO, 1930), p. 58.
37. Maria Mies, *Women: The Last Colony*, pp. 134, 136.

APPENDICES

Appendix A: Cases of Reported Rapes and Low Percentage of Convictions

Provinces	Number of Rape Cases		% of Conviction
	1880	1881	1881
North-Western Provinces & Oudh	301	334	20
Bengal	335	308	13
Panjab	111	110	42

Source: Police Reports for 1881, No. 1522A of 1882, p. 2.

Note: The Police Reports of 1915 note that the crime of rape had somewhat increased, and that it was comparatively heavier in the United Provinces of Agra and Oudh than in the adjacent provinces. The report added that the percentage of convictions continued to be low and it would always continue to be low, as false accusations were frequent (p. 18).

Appendix B:
Figures Showing the Religion and Age of All Female Convicts

	\multicolumn{8}{c}{Year}
	1878	1879	1880	1881	1882	1883	1884	1885
Religion								
European	4	0	1	1	0	0	0	0
Eurasian	2	1	0	0	0	1	1	3
Native Christians	5	0	0	1	1	3	2	0
Muslims	1,341	206	235	171	163	352	278	277
Hindus & Sikhs	9,014	1,381	1,262	1,206	1,222	2,246	2,062	1,670
Age								
Under 16	361	22	20	133	16	72	53	65
16–40	7,965	1,100	1,030	970	977	2,005	1,720	1,615
40–60	1,864	386	380	336	324	498	496	442
Over 60	166	72	60	60	69	28	34	29

	\multicolumn{8}{c}{Year}
	1891	1892	1893	1897	1898	1901	1902	1903
Religion								
European	0	0	0	0	0	0	1	0
Eurasian	0	1	1	0	0	0	0	1
Native Christians	3	2	2	3	5	1	2	1
Muslims	331	294	261	465	326	80	238	210
Hindus & Sikhs	3,430	2,729	2,324	4,921	2,461	2,731	1,665	1,618
Age								
Under 16	99	73	69	134	58	11	49	37
16–40	2,912	2,233	2,588	4,161	2,115	666	1,491	1,409
40–60	693	661	533	999	579	171	350	367
Over 60	69	59	41	95	41	6	15	17

Source: The figures have been compiled from *Jail Reports of the North-Western Provinces and Oudh*, Statement No. 11, Judicial (Criminal), showing the religion and age of convicts admitted into the jails for the years shown above.

REFERENCES

Unpublished Sources

These papers are available at the Uttar Pradesh State Archives, Lucknow.

Government of North-Western Provinces and Oudh. *Judicial (Criminal) Department Correspondence.* "The Deportation of Female Convicts to the Andamans." 1913. File No. 488/1913.

Government of North-Western Provinces and Oudh. *Judicial (Criminal) Department Notes and Orders.* "The Sale of Young Girls in Garhwal." 1908. File No. 697/1908.

Government of North-Western Provinces and Oudh. *Judicial (Criminal) Department Proceedings.* "Administration of the Police and Criminal Justice." November 1889. File No. 311B.

———. "Confinement of Prisoners Separately by Night." June 1894. File No. 378C.

———. "Deportation of Female Convicts to the Andamans." 1913. File No. 488/1913.

———. "Destruction of Records in the Criminal Courts in Oudh." January 1901. File No. 484C.

———. "Entertainment of Matrons and Female Warders." February 1888. File No. 62B.

———. "Entertainment of Matrons and Female Wardens on the Prison Staff Jails in Which Female Prisoners Are Confined." 1888. File No. 62B.

———. "Escort of the Female Prisoners to Their Homes on Release from Jail." 1886. File No. 342.

———. "Extracts from the Proceedings and the Resolutions of the Government of India in the Hone (Revenue and Agriculture) Department (Judicial) for the Years 1884, 1885, and 1900 on Cases in Which the Sentences of Transportation for Life Passed on Women for Murder of Their Infants Were Reduced or Commuted." 1901. File No. 142.

———. "Female Prisoners' Haircutting and Handcuffs." April 1894. File No. 594B.

———. "Note and Orders and Rules Regarding the Submission to Government of the Records of Cases of Women Convicted of Murdering Their Infant Children." 1899. File No. 142.

———. "Procedures to be Followed in Cases in Which Women Have Been Convicted for the Murder of Their Children Whether Legitimate or Illegitimate." 1914. File No. 87A or 1913.

———. "Proposal by the Government of India on a Bill to Make Better Provision for the Protection of Women and Girls and Other Purposes." February 1913. File No. 970 of 1912.

———. "Protection from Prostitution of Minor Girls by Means of Legislation." February 1904. File No. 669D.

———. "Question as to Whether Married Convicts Who Had Been Married in the Andamans Were Living Together." 1916. File No. 391 or 1915.
———. "Question of the Extent to Which Convict Marriages in the Andamans Are Recognized in India after the Release of the Parties." 1914. File No. 410 or 1914.
———. "Treatment of Female Prisoners in Jails in North-Western Provinces and Oudh." July 1894. File No. 252B/11.
———. "Treatment of Prisoners in Indian Jails." September 1893. File No. 122C. Government of the North-Western Provinces and Oudh. *Police Department Proceedings.* "Annual Report on Special Crime." 1889. File No. 219A; for 1890, File No. 527A; for 1892, File No. 527A/1.
———. "Enquiries into the Complaints of Police Miscon-duct." July 1912. File No. 228 of 1911.
———. "The Working of the Infanticide Act for the Years 1894-95." File No. 661A/4; for the Years 1900-1901, File No. 661/10.
Government of the North-Western Provinces and Oudh. *Revenue (Revenue) Department Proceedings.* "A Collection of Papers Connected with an Inquiry into the Conditions of the Lower Classes of the Population Especially in the Agricultural Tracts in the North-Western Provinces and Oudh." 1887–1888. File No. 753.
———. "The Reports of the Agrarian Disturbance in the Partabgarh District." 1920. File No. 753/1920.
Government of the North-Western Provinces and Oudh. *General Department: Notes and Orders.* "Dealing with Infant Marriages and Enforced Widowhood in India." 1885. File No. 408.
———. "Dealing with Infant Marriages and Enforced Widowhood in India." 1885. File No. 408/1885.
Government of the United Provinces. *Judicial (Criminal Department Proceedings.* "Bill to Suppress the Importation of Foreign Women for Prostitution." File No. 948/1912.
Singh, Priyam B., *Fiji's Indentured Labourers, 1864-1920.* Master's Thesis of Arts. Concordia University, Montreal, Canada, 1975.

OFFICIAL PUBLICATIONS I

Most of these papers are available at the National Archives of India, Delhi.

Allahabad Law Journal, Containing Cases Determined by the High Court of Allahabad. Allahabad: Government Press, 1904 to 1909.
British India (Criminal) Justice Statistical Abstract. Distribution and Number of Prisoners in North-Western Provinces and Oudh. No. 31. Thirtieth Number, 1885–1886 to 1894–1895. London: H.M.S.O., 1896.
British India (Criminal) Justice Statistical Abstract. Distribution and Number of Prisoners in North-Western Provinces and Oudh. No. Thirty-Third, 1910–1911 and preceding years. Part IV. Calcutta: Government Press, 1912.
Census of 1881. The Indian Empire Report. Vol. I. London: Eyre and Spottiswoode, 1883.
Census of India, 1891: North-Western Provinces and Oudh Report. Vol. XVI, Part 1. D. C. Baillie. Allahabad: Government Press, 1894.
Census of India, 1901: North-Western Provinces and Oudh Report. Vol. XVI, Part 1. R. Burns. Allahabad: Government Press, 1901.

REFERENCES 131

Census of India, 1921: United Provinces of Agra and Oudh Report. Part 1. E. H. H. Eyde. Allahabad: Government Press, 1923.

Collection of Papers Relating to the Condition of the Tenantry and the Working of the Present Law in Oudh. North-Western Provinces and Oudh: Government Press, 1883.

Confidential Selections from the Native Newspapers: (For the United Provinces Only). Government Press, North-Western Provinces and Oudh, 1902–1908.

Confidential Selections from the Vernacular Newspapers. Published in Punjab, North-Western Provinces and Oudh, and the Central Provinces: Government Press, 1874–1900.

Evidence Recorded by the Committee Appointed by the Government in 1890 to Enquire into Certain Questions Connected with the Police Administration of the North-Western Provinces and Oudh. Allahabad: Pioneer Press, 1891.

Indian Law Reports, Allahabad Series: Cases Determined by the High Court at Allahabad and the Judicial Committee of the Privy Council on Appeal from that Court, 1876 to 1899. Vols. I–XXI. Allahabad, 1899.

Indian Police Collection. Mss. Eur. F181. India Office Library, 1971.

Indian Statutory Commission Report (Simon Report). Vol. 1. Survey. London: H.M.S.O., 1930. (Nehru Memorial Library and Museum)

Narrative of the Famine of India, 1896-1897: Department of Revenue and Agriculture (Famine), for the Government of India. Central Printing Press, 1897.

Notes on the Administration of the Criminal Justice in the North-Western Provinces. Allahabad: Government Press, 1879–1900.

Notes on Criminal Statements of the High Court of Judicature of the North-Western Provinces for the Years 1880 and 1881. Allahabad: Government Press, 1881.

Prices and Wages in India. Compiled in the Statistical Bureau of the Government of India under the Supervision of the Director-General of Statistics. Calcutta: Office of the Superintendent of Government Printing, 1899.

Proceedings of the Government of India (Home) Department Relating to Petition for Mercy from Rahimathammal under Sentence of Death in the Madura Jail. September 1908. Nos. 113–118. From *A Collection of Important Orders and Precedents Dealing with Petition for Mercy from Convicts.* Judicial Deposit No. 6. 1885 to August 1909.

Proceedings of the Sanitary (Home) Department of the Lock Hospitals of the North-Western Provinces and Oudh for the Year 1875. Prog. Nos. 19–21, 1876.

Proceedings of the Police Department North-Western Provinces and Oudh, Enquiring into the Complaints of Police Misconduct. July 1912. File No. 228 of 1911.

Report on the Administration of the Andaman and Nicobar Islands, and the Penal Settlements of Port Blair and the Nicobars for 1878–1879. Home (Revenue and Agriculture) Department. Calcutta, 1879.

Report on the Administration of the Government of India, 1873–1874. Part 3. North-Western Provinces, Record Department. Allahabad: Government Press, 1875.

Report on the Administration of the Jails of the North-Western Provinces and Oudh. Allahabad: Government Press, 1875–1900.

Report on the Administration of the Police in the State of Uttar Pradesh (The United Provinces of Agra and Oudh) *for the Year 1959.* Uttar Pradesh: Superintendent, Printing and Stationary, 1961.

Report on the Administration of the Police of the North-Western Provinces and Oudh. Allahabad: Government Press, 1875–1915.

Report of the Administration of the United Provinces of Agra and Oudh. Allahabad: Government Press, 1903–1916.

Reports of Selected Cases Determined by the Court of Nizamut Adawlut in the North-Western Provinces. 1862–1866.

REFERENCES

Resolution on the Administration of Famine Relief in the North-Western Provinces and Oudh during 1896 and 1897. Vol. II. Allahabad: 1897.

Rules for the Management and Discipline of Prisoners in the North-Western Provinces. Allahabad: Government Press, 1874.

Weekly Notes of the Cases Decided by the High Court of the North-Western Provinces. Lucknow: Pioneer Press, 1887, 1888, and 1889.

OFFICIAL PUBLICATIONS II

District Gazetteers of the United Provinces are available at the Central Secretariat, Delhi, and Nehru Memorial Library and Museum, Delhi.

Brockman, D. (ed.), *Banda,* Vol. XXI. Allahabad, 1909.
Nevill, H. R. (ed.), *Gonda,* Vol. XLVI. Lucknow, 1905.
———. (ed.), *Agra.* Vol. VIII. Lucknow, 1908.
———. (ed.), *Allahabad.* Vol. XXIII. Allahabad, 1909.
———. (ed.), *Aligarh,* Vol. VI. Allahabad, 1909.
———. (ed.), *Ghazipur,* Vol. XXIX. Allahabad, 1909.
———. (ed.), *Pilibhit,* Vol. XVIII. Allahabad, 1909.
———. (ed.), *Shajahanpur,* Vol. XVIII. Allahabad, 1910.
———. (ed.), *Moradabad.* Vol. IX. Allahabad, 1910.
———. (ed.), *Cawnpore.* Vol. XIX. Allahabad, 1920.

STATISTICAL, DESCRIPTIVE, AND HISTORICAL ACCOUNTS OF THE NORTH-WESTERN PROVINCES OF INDIA

These are available at The Central Secretariat, Delhi.

Fisher, F. H. (ed.), *Shajahanpur.* Vol. IX, Part I. Allahabad, 1883.
———. (ed.), *Moradabad.* Vol. IX, Part II. Allahabad, 1883.
Fisher, F. H. and J. P. Hewett (eds.), *Muttra,.* Vol. VIII, Part I. Allahabad, 1884.
Fisher, F. H. and J. P. Hewett (eds.), *Allahabad.* Vol. VIII, Part II. Allahabad, 1884.
Fisher, F. H. (ed.), *Ghazipur.* Vol. XIII, Part II. Allahabad, 1884.

NEWSPAPERS AND JOURNALS

Most newspapers are available at Nehru Memorial Museum and Library, and journals at the University of Delhi.

Abhudya.
Hindi Pradeep.
Indian Antiquary.
Indian Social Reformer.
Notes and Queries: A Monthly Periodical Devoted to the Systematic Collection of Authentic Notes and Scraps of Information Regarding the Country and the People.
Pioneer.
Statesman.
Calcutta Review.
Inter Discipline, Journal of Gandhian Institute of Studies.
The Indian Journal of Social Work.

Books and Articles

A Late Indian Editor, *The Murder of Indian Judges: Showing the Causes for Disaffection in India.* London: Simpkin and Marshall, 1871.
Adam, Hargrave L., *Oriental Crime.* London: T. Werner Laurie, 1908.
———, *Woman and Crime.* London: T. Werner Laurie, 1931.
Adler, Freda, (editor), *The Incidence of Female Criminality in the World.* New York: New York University Press, 1981.
———, *Sisters in Crime: The Rise of the New Female Criminals.* New York: McGraw-Hill, 1975.
Agarwal, Vina, "Women, Poverty and Agricultural Growth in India." *The Journal of Peasant Studies.* Vol. 13, No. 4, July, 1986.
Ahuja, Ram, *Crime Against Women.* Jaipur: Rawat Publications, 1987.
———, "Female Murderers in India—A Sociological Study." *The Indian Journal of Social Work.* Vol. 31, No. 3, October, 1970: 271–284.
Anderson, Herbert, *Calcutta Vice.* Calcutta: Baptist Mission Press, 1921.
Arnold, David, "The Armed Police and Colonial Rule in South India, 1919–1947." *Modern Asian Studies.* Vol. 11, No. 1, 1977: 101-125.
———, "Bureaucratic Recruitment and Subordination in Colonial India: The Madras Constabulary, 1859–1974." *Subaltern Studies IV.* New Delhi: Oxford University Press, 1985.
———, "Dacoity and Rural Crime in Madras, 1860–1940." *The Journal of Peasant Studies.* Vol. 6, No. 2, January, 1979: 140–167.
Arnold, Sir Edwin, *The Queen's Evidence: A True Story of Indian Village Life.* London: Thomas Burleigh, 1899.
Atray, J. P., *Crimes Against Women.* New Delhi: Vikas Publishing House, 1988.
Baig, Tara Ali (editor), *Women of India.* New Delhi: Publications Division, 1958.
Baxi, Upendra, *Alternatives in Development: Law, the Crisis of the Indian Legal System.* (Indian Council of Social Science Research) New Delhi: Vikas Publishing House Pvt. Ltd., 1982.
Beattie, J. M., "The Criminality of Women in Eighteenth Century England." *Journal of Social History*, 8, 4 1975: 80–116.
Bhanu, Dharma, *History and Administration of the North-Western Provinces.* (Subsequently called the Agra Province), 1803–1858. Agra: Shiva Lal Agarwala and Co. Private Ltd., 1955.
Bhatnagar, J. P., *Offenses Against Women. (Marriage & Married Women).* Allahabad: Ashoka Law House, 1987.
Billington, M. F., *Women in India.* London: Chapman and Hall, 1895.
Bhargava, B. S., *The Criminal Tribes: A Socio-Economic Study of the Principal Criminal Tribes and Castes in Northern India.* Lucknow: Universal Publishers Ltd., 1949.
Bhattacharya, B. K., *Prisons.* Calcutta: S. C. Sarkar and Sons, 1958.
Boserup, E., *Women's Role in Economic Development.* London: Allen and Unwin, 1970.
Buyers, William, *Recollections of Northern India.* London: John Snow, Paternoster Row, 1848.
Calcutta Decennial Missionary Conference Report, *Woman's Work in the Indian Mission Field.* Calcutta: J. W. Thomas Baptist Mission Press, 1883.
Carpenter, Miss, "Our Mission Work in India," in *Note on the Jails and Jail Discipline in India,* by A. P. Howell, Under-Secretary to the Government of India. Appendix 111. Calcutta: Government Printing Press, 1868. (IOL)
Carroll, Lucy, "The Temperance Movement in India: Politics and Social Reforms." *Modern Asian Studies.* Vol. 10, No. 3, 1976: 417–447.

Chandra, Sudhir, "Literature and the Colonial Connection." *Social Scientist.* No. 121, June, 1983: 3.

———, *Social Transformation and Creative Imagination.* New Delhi: Allied Publishers Private Ltd., 1984.

Chandra, Sushil, *Sociology of Deviation in India.* Bombay, New York: Allied Publishers, 1987.

Chatterjee, Partha, "Colonialism, Nationalism, and Colonized Women: The Contest in India. The Women's Question in Tradition." *American Ethnologist.* Vol. 16, No. 4, 1989: 622–633.

Chilton, V. C., *The Sigh of the Orient.* Washington, D. C.: Review and Herald Publishing Assoc., 1924.

Cockburn, J. S. (editor), *Crime in England: 1550–1800.* New Jersey: Princeton University Press, 1977.

Cohn, Bernard S., "The British in Benares: A Nineteenth Century Colonial Society." *Comparative Studies in Society and History.* Vol. IV, No. 2. January, 1962: 168–199.

———, "Notes on the History of the Study of Indian Society and Culture." *Structure and Change in Indian Society.* Milton Singer and Bernard S. Cohn (editors). Chicago: Aldine Publishing Company, 1968.

Cooper, Elizabeth, *The Harim and the Parda: Studies of Oriental Women.* London: T. Fisher Unwin, 1915.

Cotton, Henry John Steadman, *New India or India in Transition.* London: Kegan Paul, 1907.

Cox, Sir Edmund C., *Police and Crime in India.* London: Stanley Paul and Company, n. d.

Croker, B. M., *Village Tales and Jungle Tragedies.* London: Chatto and Windus, 1895.

Crooke, William, *The Tribes and Castes of North-Western India.* Vol. 4. Calcutta: 1896; reprint ed., New Delhi: Cosmo Publications, 1975.

———, *The North-Western Provinces of India: Their History, Ethnology, and Administration.* London: Methuen and Co., 1897.

———, *Things Indian: Being Discursive Notes on Various Subjects Connected with India.* London: John Murray, 1906.

———, *Religion and Folklores of Northern India.* London: Humphrey Milford, 1926.

Curry, J. C., *The Indian Police.* London: Faber and Faber, n. d.

Dandvate, Pramila, Ranjana Kumari, and Jamila Verghese (editors), *Widows Abandoned and Destitute Women in India.* New Delhi: Radiant Publishers, 1989.

Datta, Kalinkar, *Survey of India's Social Life and Economic Condition in the Eighteenth Century (1701–1813).* Calcutta: Firma K. L. Mukhopadhyay, 1961.

Datta, V. N., *Sati: Widow Burning in India. A Historical, Social and Philosophical Enquiry into the Hindu Rite of Widow Burning.* New Delhi: Manohar Publications, 1988.

Derrett, J. Duncan M., "The Administration of Hindu Law by the British." *Comparative Studies in Society and History.* Vol. 1, No. 1, November, 1961: 10–52.

Desai, Neera, et al., "Women's Studies and the Social Sciences: A Report from India," *Women's Studies International,* No. 3, April, 1984.

Desai, N., *Women in Modern India.* Bombay: Vora, 1977.

deSouza, Alfred (editor), *Women in Contemporary India: Traditional Images and Changing Roles.* New Delhi: Manohar, 1975.

Deshpande, V. S., *Women and the New Law.* Chandigarh: Publication Bureau Punjab University, 1984.

Douglas, Hay, Peter Linebaugh, and E. P. Thompson, *Albion's Fatal Tree: Crime and*

REFERENCES • 135

Society in Eighteenth-Century England, 1859-1900. New York: Pantheon Books, 1975.
Dua, Shiva S., *Society and Culture in Northern India, 1850-1900.* New Delhi: Indian Bibliographies Bureau Co-Publisher, 1985.
Dutt, Romesh Chunder, *Famines and Land Assessments in India.* Second Print, Delhi: B. R. Publishing Corporation, 1985; First Edition, London: K. Paul, Trench, Trubner, 1900.
Dutt, Shoshee Chunder, *The Works of Shoshee Chunder Dutt. India: Past and Present, Historical and Miscellaneous.* Vol. IV, London: Lovell Reeve and Co., 1884.
Emerson, Gertrude, *Voiceless India.* Revised Edition. New York: The John Day Co., 1944.
Emsley, Clive, *Crime and Society in England: 1750-1900.* London and New York: Longman, 1987.
Etienne, Mona, and Leacock, Eleanor, (editors), *Women and Colonization: Anthropological Perspectives.* New York: Praeger Publishers, 1980.
Everett, Jana Matson, *Women and Social Change in India.* Delhi: Heritage, 1985.
Faure, Christine, "Absent from History." *Signs,* Vol. 7, No. 11 (autumn 1981-spring 1982): 71-80.
Fink, H. R., "Crimes and Punishments under Hindu Law." *Calcutta Review,* Vol. 61, 1875: 124-141.
Firestone, Shulamith, *The Dialectic of Sex: The Case for Feminist Revolution.* San Francisco: William Morrow and Company Inc., 1980.
Flax, Jane, "Postmodernism and Gender Relations in Feminist Theory." *Signs,* Vol. 12, No. 4 (summer 1987): 621-642.
Fuller, C. J., "Hinduism and Scriptural Authority in Modern Indian Law." *Comparative Studies in Society and History.* Vol. 30, No. 2 (April 1988): 225-248.
Fuller, (Mrs.) Jenny, *The Wrongs of Indian Womanhood.* Edinburgh and London: Oliphant and Co., 1900.
Gadol, Joan Kelly, "The Social Relations of the Sexes: Methodological Implications of Women's History." *Signs,* Vol. 1, No. 4, 1976: 4.
Gauba, K. L., *Famous Trials for Love and Murder.* Lahore: The Lion Press, 1945.
Ghosh, Shubhra, *Female Criminals in India: A Psychological Study of Inmates of Nari Bandi Niketan.* New Delhi: Uppal Publishing House, 1986.
Gran, Peter, *Islamic Roots of Capitalism, Egypt, 1760-1840.* Austin and London: University of Texas Press, 1979.
———, "Political Economy as a Paradigm for the Study of Islamic History" in *International Journal of Middle East Studies,* Vol. 12 (1980): 511-526.
Gray, Mrs. H., "The Progress of Women." *Modern India and the West.* L. S. S. O'Malley (editor). London: Oxford University Press, 1941.
Guha, Ranajit, *Elementary Aspects of Peasant Insurgency in Colonial India.* Delhi: Oxford University Press, 1983.
Guha, Ranajit (editor), *Subaltern Studies: Writings on South Asian History and Society.* Delhi and New York: Oxford University Press. Vol. I, 1982; Vol. II, 1983; Vol. III, 1984; Vol. IV, 1985.
Gupta, A. R., *Women in Hindu Society: A Study of Tradition and Transition.* New Delhi: Jyotsna Prakashan, 1975.
Gupta, Anandswarup, *The Police in British India: 1861-1947.* New Delhi: Concept Publishing Co., 1979.
Gurr, T. R., P. N. Grabosky, and R. C. Jula, *The Politics of Crime and Conflict: A Comparative Study of Four Cities.* Beverly Hills, California: Sage Publications, 1977.

Harding, Sandra, "The Instability of the Analytical Categories of Feminist Theory." *Signs*, Vol. 11, No. 4 (summer 1986).

Hardiman, David, "From Custom to Crime: The Politics of Drinking in Colonial South Gujarat," Ranajit Guha (editor). *Subaltern Studies IV. Writings on South Asian History and Society*. Delhi: Oxford University Press, 1985.

Hartman, Mary S., *Victorian Murderesses*. New York: SchockenBooks, 1977.

Hasunat, A., *Crime and Criminal Justice: An Outline of Criminal Sociology; Criminology; Penology; Criminal Jurisprudence and Law; and Criminal Investigation*. Dacca: Stanford Library, 1933.

Hobsbawm, Eric J., *Primitive Rebels*. New York, 1959.

Hollowell, Rev. J. Hirst, "Is India to Be Ruined by Opium?" *Brotherly Honour versus Selfish Passion: An Address to Young Men and to Citizens, on Social Purity*. London: The Moral Reform Union, n. d.

Hooja, S. L., *Dowry System in India: A Case Study*. Delhi: Asia Press, 1969.

Hunter, Sir W. W., *The Hindu Child-Widow*. Bombay: "Voice of India" Printing Press, 1887. The paper was originally contributed to the *Asiatic Quarterly Review*, October, 1886.

Immolations in India. Destruction of 1528 Females Burnt or Buried Alive in Bengal, in the Years 1815, 1816, and 1817: As Authenticated by a Copy of the Official Returns in England: With Various Arguments to Prove That These Immolations May Safely and Easily be Suppressed. London: Black, Kingsbury, Parbury, and Allen, 1821.

Indian Police Collection. Paper used by Sir Percival Griffiths to compile *To Guard My People. The History of the Indian Police*. London: 1971.

Jacobson, Doraine and Wadley, Susan S., *Women in India: Two Perspectives*. Manohar. New Delhi: 1977.

Jafri, S. N. A., *The History and Status of Landlords and Tenants in the United Provinces*. Usha Jain, 1985. (First edition, 1935.)

Jeffery, Patricia, *Frogs in a Well: Indian Women in Purdah*. London: Zed Books, 1979.

Joardar, Biswanath, *Prostitution in Historical and Modern Perspectives*. New Delhi: Inter-India Publications, 1984.

Jones, David, *Protest, Community and Police in 19th Century Britain*. London and Boston: Routledge and Kegan Paul, 1982.

Kalkar, Govind, *Women and Structural Violence in India*. Occasional Paper No. 4. Centre for Women's Development Studies. New Delhi, 1985.

Khan, Miyan Mithu, *Confessions of a Constable*. London: E. J. Lazarus and Co., 1875.

Kishwar, Madhu, and Ruth Vanita, (editors), "In Search of Answers." *Manushi*. A Collection of Articles from First Five Years of *Manushi*, 1979–1984. London: Zed Books, 1984.

Kitts, Eustace J., *Serious Crime in an Indian, Being a Record of the Graver Crime Committed in the North-Western Provinces and Oudh During Eleven Years, 1876–1886*. Bombay: Education Society's Press, 1889.

Kumar, Kapil, *Peasants in Revolt: Tenants, Landlords, Congress and the Raj in Oudh, 1886–1922*. New Delhi, Manohar, 1984.

Kumar, Pramod, "Prostitution: A Socio-Psychological Analysis." *The Indian Journal of Social Work*, Vol. 21, No. 4. March, 1961.

Larner, Christina, *Enemies of God: The Witch-hunt in Scotland*. Baltimore: Johns Hopkins University Press, 1981.

Lodha, G. M., *Deorala Fire on Pyre: Roop Kanwar's Deorala Sati Incident*. Rajasthan, 1988.

Luschinsky, Mildred Streep, "The Impact of Some Recent Indian Government Legislation on the Women on an Indian Village." *Asian Survey* Vol. 3, 1963: 573–583.

Mackinnon, Catharine A., "Feminism, Marxism, Method, and the State: An Agenda for Theory." *Signs*, Vol 7, No. 3, 1982.

———, "Feminism, Marxism, Method, and the State: Toward Feminist Jurisprudence." *Signs*, Vol. 8, No. 4, 1983.

Majumder, Niranjan, *The Statesman: An Anthology.* Calcutta and Delhi: The Statesman Ltd., 1975.

Malcolmson, R. W., "Infanticide in the Eighteenth Century," *Crime in England, 1550-1800.* J. S. Cockburn (editor). Princeton: Princeton University Press, 1977.

Mandelbaum, D.G., *Society in India, Continuity and Change.* Berkeley, Los Angeles, London: University of California Press, 1970.

Mathur, L. P., *History of the Andaman and Nicobar Islands. 1756–1966.* New Delhi, 1968.

———, *KALA PANI. History of Andaman and Nicobar Islands with a Study of India's Freedom Struggle.* New Delhi: Eastern Book Corporation, 1985.

Mazumdar, Vina (editor), "Role of Women in Development." *ICSSR.* Report of an International Seminar. New Delhi: Allied Publishers Private Ltd., 1978.

———, "Comment on Suttee." *Signs*, Vol. 4, No. 28, 1978.

Mayo, Katherine, *Mother India.* New York: Blue Ribbon Books, 1927.

———, *Slaves of the Gods.* New York: Harcourt, Brace and Company, 1929.

Mies, Maria, *The Lacemakers of Narsapur: Indian Housewives Produce for the World Market.* London: Zed Books Ltd., 1982.

———, *Indian Women and Patriarchy.* New Delhi: Concept Publishing Company, 1980.

Mies, Maria; Veronika Bennholdt-Thomsen, and Claudia von Werlhof, *Women: The Last Colony.* London: Zed Books Ltd., 1988.

Miller, Barbara D., *The Endangered Sex: Neglect of Female Children in Rural North India.* Ithaca: Cornell University Press, 1981.

Mitchell, Juliet, *Woman's Estate.* New York: Vintage Books, 1973.

Morrison, Rev. John, *New Ideas in India During the Nine-teenth Century: A Study of Social, Political, and Religious Developments.* Edinburgh: George A. Martin, 1906.

Mittal, S. K. and K. Kumar, "Baba Ram Chandra and Peasant Upsurge in Oudh, 1920–1921." *Social Scientist,* June 1978.

Mullick, Bulloo Ram, (Mallika Balarama), *Essays on Hindu Family in Bengal.* Calcutta: W. Newman & Co., Limited, 1882.

Nandy, Ashis, *At the Edge of Psychology. Essays in Politics and Culture.* Delhi: Oxford University Press, 1980.

Nesfield, John Collinson, (Inspector of Schools), *Brief View of the Caste System of the North-Western Provinces and Oudh, Together with an Examination of Names and Figures Shown in the Census Report, 1882, Being an Attempt to Classify on a Functional Basis All the Main Castes of U. P.* Allahabad: Government Press, 1885.

Nye, Robert, "Crime in Modern Societies: Some Research Strategies for Historians." *Journal of Social History*, Vol. 11, No. 4, 1978: 493.

O'Brien, Patricia, "Crime and Punishment as Historical Problem." *Journal of Social History*, Vol. 11, No. 4, 1978: 508–520.

———, *The Promise of Punishment: The Prisons in Nineteenth-Century France.* Princeton, N. J.: Princeton University Press, 1982.

O'Connor, Percival C. Scott, *The Indian Countryside, A Calendar and Diary.* London: Brown Langham and Co., 1907.

REFERENCES

O'Malley, L. S. S. (editor), *Modern India and the West. A Study of the Interaction of Their Civilizations.* London: Oxford University Press, 1941.

Omvedt, Gail, *We Will Smash This Prison! Indian Women in Struggle.* London: Zed Books Ltd., 1980.

———, "Patriarchy: The Analysis of Women's Oppression," *The Insurgent Sociologist,* Vol. 13, No. 3, spring 1986.

———, "Migration in Colonial India: The Articulation of Feudalism and Capitalism by the Colonial State," *The Journal of Peasant Studies,* Vol. 7, No. 2. January 1980.

"On the Benefits Arising to the Military Service from Abstinence Societies," by an Officer, in *A Plea for the British Soldier in India.* London: William Tweedie, 1867.

Peggs, James, *India Cries to British Humanity Relative to Infanticide.* London: Simpkin and Marshall, 1832.

Perrot, Michelle, "Delinquency and the Penitentiary Systems in the Nineteenth Century," in *Deviants and the Abandoned in French Society: Selections from the Annales Economies, Societies, Civilisations,* Vol. 4. Robert Forster and Orest Ranum (editors). Baltimore, 1978.

Pinch, Trevor, *Stark India.* New York: D. Appleton and Co., 1931.

Rafter, Nicole H., and Elizabeth A. Stanko, *Judge, Lawyer, Victim, Thief: Women, Gender, Roles, and Criminal Justice.* Northeastern University, 1982.

Raj, Jagdish, *Economic Conflict in Northern India: A Study of Landlord-Tenant Relations in Oudh: 1970–1890.* Bombay: Allied Publishers Private Limited, 1978.

Ramabai, Sarasvati Pandita, *The High-Caste Hindu Woman.* Second Edition. New Delhi: Inter-India Publications, 1984; first edition, Philadelphia, 1887.

Rao, Ragonatha D. B. R., "Punishment by Imprisonment." *The Pioneer,* Lucknow: May 10, 1890. (Reprinted from a Madras paper.)

Rao, Venugopal S., *Facets of Crime in India.* Second Edition. New Delhi: Allied Publishers Private Ltd., 1967.

Rao, V., *Dynamics of Crime: Spatial and Socio-Economic Aspects of Crime in India.* New Delhi: Indian Institute of Public Administration, 1981.

Rau, Bill, *From Feast to Famine: Official Cures and Grassroots Remedies to Africa's Food Crisis.* London: Zed Books Ltd., 1991.

Richardson, Laurel, and Taylor, Verta, *Feminist Frontiers: Rethinking Sex, Gender, and Society.* Massachusetts: Addison-Wesley Publishing Company, 1983.

Roy, Jaytilak G., *Prisons and Society: A Study of the Indian Jail System.* New Delhi: Gian Publishing House, 1989.

Sacks, Karen, "State Bias and Women's Status." *American Anthropologist,* Vol. 78, No. 3, 1976: 565–569.

———, *Sisters and Wives. The Past and Future of Sexual Equality.* Chicago: University of Illinois Press, 1982.

Samuelson, James, *India, Past and Present: Historical, Social and Political.* London: Trubner and Co., 1890.

Sangar, Satya Prakash, *Crime and Punishment in Mughal India.* Delhi: Sterling Publishers Ltd., 1967.

Sangari, Kumkum, and Sudesh Vaid, (editors), *Recasting Women, Essays in Colonial History.* New Delhi: Kali for Women, 1989.

Schulte, Regina, "Infanticide in Rural Bavaria in the Nineteenth Century." *Interest and Emotion: Essays in the Study of Family and Kinship.* Hans Medick and David Warren Sabean (editors). London, New York: Cambridge University Press, 1984.

Sharma, Arvind, "Hindu Religious Reformers as Feminists: Paradox or Hypocracy." *Asian Profile*, Vol. 11, No. 2. April 1983.
Sharma, Miriam, "Caste, Class, and Gender: Production and Reproduction in North India." *The Journal of Peasants Studies*, Vol. 12, No. 4. July 1985: 57–87.
Sharpe, J. A., "The History of Crime in Late Medieval England: A Review of the Field." *Social History*, Vol. 7, No. 2, 1982: 182–203.
Singer, Milton and Bernard S. Cohn (editors), *Structure and Change in Indian Society*. Chicago: Aldine Publishing Company, 1968.
Singh, Iqbal N., *The Andaman Story*. New Delhi: Vikas Publishing House Private Ltd., 1978.
Sohani, Neera K., *Women Behind Bars*. New Delhi: Vikas Publishing House Pvt. Ltd., 1989.
Sohani, N. K., "Women Prisoners." *The Indian Journal of Social Work*, Vol. 35, No. 2, 1947a: 137–148.
———, "A Profile of Women Prisoners in India." *Inter Discipline: Journal of Gandhian Institute of Studies*, Vol. 2, No. 2 (summer 1974): 30–52.
Somerville, Augustus, *Crime and Religious Beliefs in India*. Calcutta: W. Newman and Co. Ltd., 1929.
Spivak, Gayatri Chakravorty, *In Other Worlds: Essays in Cultural Politics*. New York and London: Methuen, 1987.
———, "Discussion-Subaltern Studies: Deconstructing Historiography." *Subaltern Studies IV*. Ranajit Guha (editor). Delhi, 1985.
Srinivas, M. N., *The Remembered Village*. Berkeley, Los Angeles and London: University of California Press, 1980.
Srivastava, Dharma Bhanu, *The Province of Agra: Its History and Administration* (second revised edition). New Delhi: Concept, 1979. First published in 1957.
Starchey, Sir John, *India: Its Administration and Progress*. London: MacMillan and Co., 1911.
Stavrianos, L. S., *Global Rift: The Third World Comes of Age*. New York: William Morrow and Company, Inc., 1981.
Stein, Dorothy, "Women to Burn: Suttee as a Normative Institution." *Signs*, Vol. 4, No. 2 (August 1978–September 1979): 253–267.
Tek, Chand and Sarin, H. L., *The Child Marriage Restraint Act*. Calcutta: Eastern Law House, 1939.
The Christian Vernacular Education Society, *The Women of India and What Can Be Done for Them. Papers on Indian Reform*. Vepery: S. P. C. R. Press, 1888.
Temple, Colonel, "The Women of India." A Paper Read to the Parliamentary Committee for Women's Suffrage. March 8, 1899.
Thesiger, Frederick, "Abstinence in the Army," *Tracts on the Drink Question. A Plea for the British Soldier in India*. Agra Soldiers' Total Abstinence Association. London: William Tweedie, 1867.
Tobias, J. J., *Crime and Industrial Society in the 19th Century*. New York: Schocken Books, 1986.
Thomas, P., *Woman and Marriage in India*. London: George Allen and Unwin, 1939.
Wadley, Susan Snow, *Shakti: Power in the Conceptual Structure of Karimpur Religion*. The University of Chicago Studies in Anthropology Series in Social, Cultural and Linguistic Anthropology. The University of Chicago, 1975.
Walsh, Sir Cecil Henry, *The Agra Double Murder*. London: Ernest Benn Ltd., 1929.
Walsh, C. H., *Crime in India with an Introduction of Forensic Difficulties and Peculiarities*. London: Ernest Benn, 1932.

———, *Indian Village Crime*. London: Ernest Benn, 1932.

Ward Gailey, Christine, *Kinship to Kingship. Gender Hierarchy and State Formation in the Tongan Islands*. Austin: University of Texas Press, 1987.

Washbrook, D. A., "Law, State and Agrarian Society in Colonial India." *Modern Asian Studies*, Vol. 15, No. 3, 1981: 649–654.

Whitcombe, Elizabeth, *Agrarian Conditions in Northern India. Volume 1. The United Provinces Under British Rule, 1860–1900*. Berkeley, Los Angeles, London: University of California Press, 1972.

Woman's Work in the Indian Mission Field. Reprinted from the Report of the Calcutta Decennial Missionary Conference. Calcutta: J. W. Thomas, Baptist Mission Press, 1883.

"World Citizen," *Sister India: A Critical Examination of and a Reasoned Reply to Miss Katherine Mayo's Other India*. Bombay: n. d.

Yang, Anand, (editor), *Crime and Criminality in British India*. Tucson: University of Arizona Press, 1985.

INDEX

Adultery, 31, 53, 70, 89, 99, 119
Abuse, victimization, oppression, xi, xii, 7, 20, 82, 84, 95, 98, 99, 109, 110, 111, 117, 119, 121, 127
Ahirs, 87
Andaman and the Nicobar Islands, 33, 38, 48, 57, 72, 108, 109, 115, 122
Appeasement policy, 18, 19, 70, 73, 82, 90, 119

Bania, 19
Bhangis, 33, 87, 60
Battered women syndrome, xii, 73
Brahman (or Brahmin), 35, 61, 63, 65, 66, 72, 89, 119
Born criminals, 2, 32
British soldiers, 81, 82, 83, 84, 85, 86
Cantonments, 8, 81, 84, 85, 86, 89, 121, 123
Carpenter's report, 101, 102, 103
Caste, 1, 6, 7, 35, 51, 111, 121, 124
Chamar, 60
Chaukidar, 37, 56, 97, 99, 100, 122
Child-marriage, 1, 6, 8, 9, 58, 59, 60, 61, 62, 63, 66, 70, 97
Child-widows, 60, 61, 107, 108, 109, 110
Code of criminal procedure, 19
Collusion of colonial rulers and high-caste native patriarchs, xi, 3, 8, 15, 19, 21, 32, 33, 34, 47, 51, 72, 73, 97, 108, 113, 119
Colonial culture against women, xii, 65, 72, 81, 83, 97, 117, 123, 124
Colonial justice, xi, 1, 2, 4, 36, 53, 54, 62, 65, 66, 70, 84, 95, 97, 100, 122
Colonial revenue, 19, 86, 87, 88
Commercialization of agriculture, 7, 18, 26, 28, 30, 36, 38, 86, 121
Concubinage, 66, 67
Concubine, 63, 67

Conjugal rights, 53, 96
Contagious Diseases Act, 85, 86, 90
Crime, xii, 3, 4, 15, 21, 22, 25, 26, 33, 34, 36, 37, 32, 39, 47, 70, 72, 82, 87, 97, 98, 110, 111, 119, 120, 122
Criminal tribes, 5, 36, 37

Dakait (or Dacoit), 5, 97, 99
Deshmukh, Gopal Hari, 62
Divide and rule, 82, 83, 84, 90, 95
Domestic violence, 48, 51, 52, 53, 54, 55, 56, 57, 89, 96, 97, 119
Drowning, 54, 55, 56, 57, 119

Economic deprivation, 1, 15, 16, 18, 19, 20, 21, 25, 26, 28, 29, 31, 32, 33, 34, 59
Elliot, Sir Charles, 23
Emigration, 7, 18, 29, 32, 38, 81, 88, 118, 121, 123
Enforced widowhood, 1, 6, 8, 16, 25, 57, 58, 60, 61, 62, 97

Famines, 7, 15, 16, 25, 28, 29, 31, 118
Female convicts, 15, 16, 17, 18, 49, 69, 95, 106, 107, 108, 109, 111, 127
Female ex-convicts, 103, 105, 106, 107, 108, 111, 123

Gandhi, Mahatama, 71
Grave and sudden provocation, 53, 96

Harijan, 6
Hindu women, 1, 2, 5, 6, 50, 51, 52, 72, 96, 117, 119, 124
Hindu mother-in-law, 51, 58, 118
Hunter, Sir W. W., 23

Immoral lower castes, 31, 51, 82, 83, 84, 118

INDEX

Imperial interests, 19, 80, 90, 108, 111, 118, 122
Incest, xi, 64, 67, 70
Indian Penal Code, 55
Infanticide, 1, 120
Infanticidal widows, 64, 65
Inquiry of 1882, 30
Inquiry of 1886, 21
Inquiry of 1888, 21, 23, 25
Izzat, 98

Kidnapping, 15, 35, 88, 89

Lathi, 53
Lower immoral castes, 2, 7, 31, 37, 39, 60, 61, 82, 83, 84, 121, 122, 124
Luddoo, 19

Malabari, Mr., 61, 68
Marriage Legislation of 1860, 61
Mayo, Katherine, 60, 61
Mehta, 21
Missionaries, 43, 51
Mother murderesses, 33, 34, 55, 56, 57, 64, 65, 68, 123
Modernization and moralization, 1, 18, 38, 67, 70, 81, 85, 112, 120
Mughal, 19, 101
Murderesses, 5, 31, 32, 64, 68, 71, 118, 119
Murder-suicide, 55, 56, 118
Mutiny, 5, 9, 18, 66, 119

Non-Interference Clause of the Regulation of 1793, 64, 65, 66, 73, 97, 120

Ostracism, 75, 95, 100, 119, 123

Panchayat, 7, 61, 75, 100
Patriarchy, xi, 3, 1, 3, 9, 13, 47, 48, 50, 53, 59, 61, 73, 90, 96, 124, 218
Penal system, 9, 100, 109
Police, 97, 98, 99, 100, 107, 124
Police Inquiry of 1891 and 1912, 98
Prison, 18, 47, 101, 102, 103, 104, 105, 107, 111, 112
Population, 24, 25, 26, 29, 30, 61, 62
Prostitutes, 32, 51, 51, 85, 89, 102, 104, 107, 121

Prostitution, 67, 85, 89, 102, 111, 119, 120, 122
Pundit, 63
Punishment, xii, 4, 5, 18, 26, 47, 48, 64, 97, 100, 101
Purdah system, 98, 118

Raj, xi, 4, 5, 65
Ramabai, Pandita Sarasvati, 58, 78
Rao, Sir Madhava, 64
Rape, 64, 82, 99, 100, 128
Recruiters, 88, 89
Religious ideology, 4, 5, 47, 57, 58, 120
Reform, 9, 53, 63, 65, 72, 88, 103, 112, 120
Respectable higher castes, 2, 35, 50, 63, 66, 67, 72, 82, 84
Respectability, 1, 36, 59, 61, 72, 82, 90, 91
Right of Maintenance, 59

Salvation Army, 45
Sati (or Suttee), 1, 6, 8, 57, 59, 65, 71 123
Sedition Act, 84
Sessions Judges, 54, 99
Sexual exploitation, 31, 39, 50, 59, 71, 84, 88, 121
Sexual jealousies, 121
Sudras, 6 25, 89
Suicide, 15, 32, 33, 48, 54, 55, 56, 57

Talookdar, 18
Temperance Movement, 87
Thagi, 95
Toddy, 87
Transportation of women to British colonies and penal colonies, 9, 64, 84, 95, 108, 111

Vidyasagara, Ishwara Chandra, 60, 62
Violence against women, 52, 53, 83, 86, 87, 89, 90

Widowers, 58, 59, 60, 62
Widows, 8, 57, 58, 59, 62, 63, 64, 65, 67, 68, 70, 71, 72, 119, 123
Widow Remarriage Act of 1856, 62, 63
Widow-remarriage, 9, 53, 57, 62, 63, 66, 70,

Women's crimes, 67, 68, 70, 71, 73
Women, executed, 56, 80, 81, 82, 83, 130
Women kidnappers, 15, 35, 119
Women oppressors, 51, 58, 118
Women poisoners, 15, 34, 35, 119

Women victims or criminals, xi, xii, 1, 5, 7, 20, 29, 31, 32, 33, 34, 35, 39, 47, 48, 55, 64, 68, 70, 81, 82, 84, 99, 102, 107, 109, 110, 117, 121, 123, 124

Zanana, 98